In Cara the unique and beautiful shape of one child's life is displayed – part of the stunning patchwork of individual stories about people with disabilities and their families. For parents, professionals, volunteers and churches, read and see; catch a vision of the need and the love, and then act in the light of it.

*Sally Hodges, parent of a son with disabilities and Nottingham Mencap Trustee*

*Cara: A hope and a future* is a moving personal story told in a vivid and forceful way. It contains very helpful reflections, especially on suffering and caring for a disabled child, where the author's insights reveal a high degree of acceptance and maturity. No doubt she has learnt them in the difficult arena of her own painful experience. The spontaneous mixture of the two main issues of the work – suffering and the struggle for social justice to help the disabled – makes it an original and highly recommendable read.

*Dr Pablo Martinez, psychiatrist and writer*

Grittily honest and devoid of sentimentality, yet totally life affirming. Rhona has managed to write a very readable book interweaving her spiritual journey with the practical challenges of parenting her disabled daughter. This could potentially be a depressing book highlighting the all-too-familiar problems of trying to get the help promised by statutory agencies and dealing with the misunderstanding of friends, but despite this, the author has imbued the book with hope. It should not just be read by parents who identify with the subject, but by all who care enough to understand more about living with or being affected by disability in today's world.

*Jacky Oliver, Chief Executive, Through the Roof: Through the Roof has a vision to see all disabled people reach their full God-given potential*

D1103157

# Cara

Rhona J. Tolchard

# Cara

## A hope and a future

ivp

INTER-VARSITY PRESS
Norton Street, Nottingham NG7 3HR, England
Email: ivp@ivpbooks.com
Website: www.ivpbooks.com

The views and opinions expressed in this work are solely those of the author and do not necessarily reflect those of the publishers.

*First published 2010*

**British Library Cataloguing in Publication Data**
A catalogue record for this book is available from the British Library.

ISBN 978–1–84474–430–5

Set in 11.5/14pt Chaparral
Typeset in Great Britain by CRB Associates, Potterhanworth, Lincolnshire
Printed in Great Britain by Ashford Colour Press Ltd, Gosport, Hampshire

*Inter-Varsity Press publishes Christian books that are true to the Bible and that communicate the gospel, develop discipleship and strengthen the church for its mission in the world.*

*Inter-Varsity Press is closely linked with the Universities and Colleges Christian Fellowship, a student movement connecting Christian Unions in universities and colleges throughout Great Britain, and a member movement of the International Fellowship of Evangelical Students. Website: www.uccf.org.uk*

For both my families,
at home and at church

# Contents

# Acknowledgments

There are many individuals who supported us during the Cara years:

Cara's volunteers, too many to mention by name, who showed so much devotion to helping her; we are more grateful than we can ever express and we will always remember your commitment in giving Cara some of the happiest years of her life.

Those professionals working within the system who understood what we were trying to do and did their absolute best to help us, especially Rebecca Billard, Judith James, Dr Helen Leonard, Professor Gordon Dutton, Avril Godfrey and Ruth Masters.

Our two childminders, Susan Michinson and Janet McCree, who helped us hold things together, and Cara's social services careworkers, whose kindness helped our whole family, not just Cara.

Those who gave us unstinting support at the sharp end, especially Claire Jackson and Dawn Kelly, who continue to fight the good fight on behalf of their own children.

Those who cared for Cara and us at the end of her life at the Paediatric Intensive Care Unit, Newcastle General Hospital.

Kathryn, Rachel and Fiona, my prayer group, for spirituality, girl talk, coffee and great cakes, and 'the clan', our house group, for many evenings of seriousness and hilarity. I am also grateful to the Rev. David Day for his support and encouragement in the writing of this book and to everyone at IVP for taking on a challenging project (the book and me). Lastly, I thank the clergy, staff and congregation of St Nicholas's Church, Durham, who continue to show us the meaning of Christian community.

# Preface

Some years ago, when our daughter Cara was very small, I first had the idea of writing a book about her and about our life with her. I envisaged it as a Christian book that would tell a story about how God intervened to help us help our daughter and about some of the things we did to make her better. However, as she grew older, the story became a lot more complicated, and we learned lots of new things – about ourselves, about the complexity of God's purposes and about the injustice that exists in the world towards disabled people and towards severely disabled children in particular.

In a way, this book is a last resort, an attempt to raise issues that we were unable to raise effectively during Cara's lifetime, and even after her death, because no-one in the system was sufficiently interested. If the function of the law is to achieve a balance of interests between different groups of people in society, then from our experience, the balance is tipped heavily against disabled children and their families. The book is an attempt to increase understanding about the effects of severe disability and about the issues facing the families of disabled children everywhere in this country and at this time. My understanding, from speaking to education and legal professionals, is that it seems to be the case that the more profoundly disabled children are, the less chance they have of reasonable educational opportunity in relation to their disability and the less chance their parents have of being taken seriously when they question what is happening. That is what we found out through personal experience and this seems to me to be discriminatory and to need addressing.

Because this is still primarily a Christian book, it is also an account of the spiritual journey undertaken by our family, of the way in which God moved in our lives and of the way in which our hope and trust in him kept us going through some unbelievably hard times. It is written for all those who feel that the world is threatening to swallow them up and that the pressures of life are too much for them. For everyone at this point, Jesus is eternally present, offering hope and renewal.

'I know the plans I have for you . . . plans to prosper you and not to harm you, plans to give you hope and a future' (Jeremiah 29:11).

# Part 1

# Beginnings and Endings

# 1  A New Life

That Thursday morning in August began like so many others – with Cara having a seizure. Usually, she would cry out as it began, with a particular cry that we knew only too well, but lately there had been no cries. The seizure must have begun a while before, maybe even while she was still asleep, because it was already well established when we went in, but David and I kicked straight into action: he went downstairs to get the paraldehyde while I stayed with her, and then when he came back, I phoned for the ambulance. By this time Cara's social services helpers had arrived; Linda helped David by lifting Cara so that he could administer the drug, while Allison stayed downstairs with our younger daughter to wait for the ambulance.

They arrived – and took her straight to hospital after trying unsuccessfully to bring her out of the seizure. Because she was still in it, David went in the ambulance with her.

I wasn't any more worried than I usually was when this happened. Instead I carried on as normal: gave Charis her breakfast and dressed her, and when her childminder Janet arrived, told her what had happened and sent her off.

I immediately stripped Cara's bed, because paraldehyde smells appalling (like rotting hazelnuts), opened the window wide and threw the bedding straight into the washing machine. I rinsed out the syringes and then made up Cara's bed again. She would probably be back this evening or tomorrow. This was routine. Although it was always upsetting, it was manageable.

I was well into doing the housework when the telephone rang at about ten o'clock. I knew that it would be David, but I wasn't prepared for what he told me.

'I need you here; call your mum and tell her to get a taxi. Has Charis gone?'

'Yes, but why do you need me?'

David said, very matter-of-factly, 'She arrested and they had to resuscitate her. You need to be here.'

I did as he asked and, after waiting much too long for a taxi, met him in Accident and Emergency at Sunderland Royal. By that time, they were getting ready to send Cara to the General Hospital in Newcastle. I saw her lying flat on the trolley, covered in tubes and bleeding badly from the nose where they had inserted her breathing tube. One of the doctors explained to me that it was because she probably had quite large adenoids. I answered rationally, because we were both very used to medical/therapeutic discussions about Cara. They wouldn't let me touch her because they were still trying to stabilize her. She looked like the victim of a very bad accident.

Looking back now, I find it hard to understand how I stayed so calm or how I didn't identify even now that this time was different. Nine and a half years of living with epilepsy, of uncertain medical prognoses, of struggles with the education authority and with the occupational therapy department had meant that both David and I were inured to crisis and conflict and well schooled in self-control and patience. Perhaps it was shell shock, perhaps endurance, or perhaps a bit of both. Even as I write now, I find it hard to be emotional about this part of the story.

When we got to the hospital, we found that we had got there before the ambulance. As we entered the building, for the first time a sliver of panic penetrated my defences. The last time we had been here was when Cara was diagnosed, four months after her birth, and it had been unimaginably terrible. I made myself concentrate on what was happening now. The Paediatric Intensive Care Unit was beautifully decorated (we had, at least, never been here before), with a frieze of the story of Noah's Ark in the corridor; when Cara finally arrived, we settled in to await whatever would come.

The old nervous reaction to dry, academic doctors with scary diagnoses was still with me, as it always had been since the early days with Cara, so, after our first encounter with the consultant on duty, who pulled no punches as to how serious this was, I left most of the other interviews to David. By this time, however, I was less intimidated than I had been at the beginning, because I had had plenty of practice, and as always, we slipped into coping mode. My mother stayed at home looking after Charis; David's mother spent some time at the hospital with us. The rest of the time we spent chatting with the nurses and talking to Cara, trying to encourage her to come back to us.

It all sounds bizarrely normal and it was, though it was punctuated with tears and moments of despair. On that first day, there was some hope, which lasted through Friday, and we called Charis's minder and our house group leader to ask for prayers to be said at the two churches with which our family had been associated. We had been told that the first forty-eight hours were significant and that all the unit could do was to support Cara's body while, as the doctors put it, she 'decided' whether or not she was able to take over again. We swung up and down and back and forth, those two days, watching the numbers on her life support, watching the nurses come and go adjusting the dosages, watching the plasma slowly dripping into her bloodstream to help her failing liver. Oddly enough, I can't remember feeling afraid when I was with her. The fears came when I was watching the doctors with her or when I left to get a cup of tea and had to come back; towards the end of our vigil, I had to make my feet step one in front of the other, and the patterned linoleum on the way into the unit became for me a road marked with suffering.

But once I was there, that disappeared. I talked to Cara. Stroked her hair, held her hand, which she never allowed me to do when conscious, told her how much we loved and missed her and wanted her to come back. At the same time, as the hours drew on, a slow and unemotional conviction began to grow in me that she probably wouldn't this time, though neither David nor I mentioned it to each other. As always, we concentrated on the next hour, the next task.

At about midnight, one of the curates from St Nicholas's, who had been told about the situation by our house group leader, came to pray with us. The nurses kept a respectful distance as he laid hands on Cara.

'What do you want me to pray for?' he asked me.

I hesitated. 'I want what's best for Cara, whatever that is,' I said, through my tears.

He looked at Cara on the bed, wired up, bloody still because she now no longer had enough clotting agent to stem the bleeding from her nose and neck. 'She's had a hard time, hasn't she?' he said gently.

We held hands around the bed and prayed for her, committing her to God, and for a few minutes the bedside became a palpably holy place, light, silent and peaceful, and shot through with the presence of Jesus. The peace that Peter brought with him stayed with us and lapped around the edges of our anguish, so that we seemed to be held on an island in a deep sea of hope and love and certainty.

The hours passed. We went away and came back again, and took it in turns to spend time with Cara. When it was my turn, I talked to her again. I had read somewhere that children are often afraid to die because they worry about how their families will cope without them.

'You know,' I whispered, 'if you really want to go and be with God, it's OK. We will manage; don't worry about us. You do what you want to do.'

The time continued to pass. Sometime that afternoon, one of the consultants came and examined Cara's readings. She said that they were showing a negative trend and that she was not showing any real sign of recovery. When she left, I went back to talk to Cara. 'Well, so you've made your decision then,' I said.

The tears flowed at intervals throughout the rest of that day, yet we were still able to laugh and joke with the nurses as they came and went. One girl had plaited Cara's hair in scalp plaits the previous night while on duty and she looked beautiful, lying there, a sleeping princess, a young girl on the verge of womanhood, tall, straight, well proportioned despite her disability, her long dark lashes sweeping her cheeks. I had a picture in my head, as I watched her, of Cara as she should have been: a shy, dreamy little girl who loved music, with a wicked sense of humour, placid and softly spoken.

As we laughed and chatted around her, I didn't realize what David had already guessed – that Cara had already slipped away from us and that it was only the machines and the medication that were keeping her body functioning. Life on the ward continued around us in our little family unit, but she was no longer there. Even at this point, however, the doctors were still working away, continuing to give her blood, using some very expensive drugs, even telephoning one of the large London hospitals to find out how to help her recover liver function. There was for us, afterwards, a sense of irony that the levels of care and expertise that had been missing for most of Cara's life were now being given to her at the end of it, but we were nevertheless grateful for everything they tried to do.

The night wore on. David took me home so that I could get some sleep, and a friend of my mother's drove me back in the morning. It took every ounce of strength I had to go back on to the ward, but I made it. I slipped out to go to Communion in the hospital chapel, and came back. Still no changes and no decision.

The senior consultant, Dr Mistry, had decided to do a brain scan to check for activity, but because it was a Sunday it took some time to find a neurologist and a portable machine. At four o'clock the scan was done and it confirmed what David already knew – that there was no brain activity and that Cara was being maintained artificially. Dr Mistry brought us into a small consultation room, and with honesty but also with great kindness, told us that there was therefore no purpose in keeping her alive, and so we went back for a final time while the nurses drew the screens around the bed and began to remove the tubes. We stood on either side of her, holding her hands as they switched everything off, leaving us alone with her as her body finally let her spirit go.

We had both been there when she was born and we were both privileged to be there when she passed. She was born on a Sunday and she died on a Sunday with much less pain and effort; I had been terrified that she would convulse and gasp for breath, but it was utterly peaceful: her heart simply slowed and then quietly stopped. It was half past four on Sunday 26 August 2007 and my daughter was finally free. When we talked about it afterwards, we decided that she had been smarter than any of us; God had given her the chance to go and she had taken it without any struggle. A pure heart and a gentle spirit, she would finally be able to do all the things that had been denied to her on earth, not only by her physical and mental disabilities, but also by flawed human beings. I thought of Dietrich Bonhoeffer's last words: 'This is the end; for me, the beginning of life.'[1]

It was a warm, sunny evening. As I stepped outside the hospital, I met a relative of another child in the Intensive Care Unit, a little Muslim boy who was to go back on to the regular ward. I smiled and asked how he was: he said that the child was doing well. 'And – your daughter?' I shook my head. I thanked him for the kindness the child's family had shown to us. They were from the Bangladeshi community in Sunderland, people who normally keep very much to themselves, but an unlikely camaraderie had grown up between us during our respective days of crisis. As the child's father had said to my mother and me on one occasion, no matter who or what we are, we all have the same concerns as human beings and we all feel the same pain.

I had dreaded this moment from the beginning of Cara's problems with epilepsy: the seizure she did not come out of. Yet now that it had happened, although the pain and shock were deep, we did not mourn without hope, and in an odd way for such a young person, there was a sense of completion about Cara's death, a peace, a rightness. For nine and a half years, she had been our family's heartbeat, but now her work was done and her struggles were over. The life she had left had been so limited that no-one could possibly have wished her back into it. And the faith that had grown throughout our years with her now supported us and gave us the absolute assurance that this was not a final parting and that we would see her again. It had not always been so.

## 2 An Injured Family

I have always had a very good memory. Details of speech in particular, but also of people's dress and mannerisms, stick in my mind; I carry a vast and untidy portmanteau of useless facts in my head that somehow stay there to be unearthed on the rare occasions when they are needed. However, when I think back to the time when all our lives were irrevocably changed, my memory resists, unwilling to revisit the facts that provoked such painful feelings at the time.

Cara was our first child and the child I thought I might never have. I had married first in my late twenties, but it had ended in divorce soon afterwards. David and I were married when I was thirty-four, so we knew that if we wanted children, we needed to start straight away. We spent two years trying to no avail, but finally I managed to conceive naturally while waiting for fertility treatment. I proudly wore my maternity clothes, planned colour schemes and fitments for the nursery, and even coped with dreadful morning sickness. Otherwise, the pregnancy was completely uneventful and gave no indication at all of what was to come. I worked until I reached six months, then happily finished and enjoyed a pregnant Christmas and a New Year (1998) filled with promise.

We did not choose a girl's name until three weeks before my due date. Because my twenty-week scan had shown a big baby, with big feet, I was convinced it was a boy (in those days it was not a matter of routine to tell parents the baby's sex). Then when we couldn't think of a name we both liked enough, I went to our local library and borrowed a book of babies' names. We chose Cara eventually, for a variety of reasons; it was Celtic, and my ancestry is mostly Scottish; it means 'beloved' in Latin and in Italian, and 'friend' in Irish. We followed it with Joanna, the Latinized version of my mother's name, and finally with Fay simply because David liked it.

Towards the end of the pregnancy, the sickness returned, and now the midwife began to be worried about me because my blood pressure was steadily rising. My ankles swelled so that I couldn't fit into my shoes. The baby's due date came and went; days followed with no sign of labour starting. I have a family history of pre-eclampsia, so I now had to check into the antenatal monitoring unit at the hospital. They admitted me for a weekend, then released me, and still the baby didn't come. My midwife checked my blood pressure twice a day and shook her head at the doctors having sent me home. One Friday, she telephoned the hospital saying that they had to admit me. We drove to the hospital but were told that they were unable to induce me as they were already fully booked, at which point I began to get very nervous indeed. Finally, after David lost his temper with the doctor on duty, they agreed to admit me for an induced labour, much to everyone's relief.

Nothing, least of all my cosy antenatal classes that talked about minimal pain relief and active labour, had prepared me for how it would be. It was started on the Friday night. David had gone home and I was left by myself with my TENS pain-relief machine for company, stifling my moans in case I woke the others on the antenatal ward, unable to sleep and beginning to be scared of what was going to happen.

David arrived the following morning, and my labour continued all day Saturday and most of Saturday night. As I finally reached stage two, I was exhausted, even with an epidural, and as I lay there, I wondered whether or not I was going to die, before deciding that if I did, I didn't really care all that much. We progressed to forceps and then to the possibility of an emergency Caesarean section if I couldn't push harder. The way it was described made it sound threatening; the doctor in charge looked tired and sounded grumpy. Finally, Cara was hauled out, screaming with pain and cut on the forehead, but alive and, to us, beautiful, huge (9 lb 5 oz) and, as far as anyone could tell, absolutely perfect. It was finally over, and the elation hit me even in my state of desperate tiredness and massive blood loss. As they were stitching me up, I spoke excitedly to my mother on the phone. It was twenty minutes after midnight on Sunday 1 March, and we were parents at last.

As I lay in bed on the ward with my baby beside me several hours later, one of the midwives on duty popped her head round the curtain to look at us. She checked me and then the baby.

'I just need to take the baby away for a minute, Rhona – won't be long,' she said, and whisked Cara away. A few minutes later, she returned. I lay watching her face, barely registering what she was telling me.

'I'm afraid the baby's stopped breathing, Rhona, so we've taken her into the neonatal unit. We've sent for your husband; it's probably nothing but we do need to check her out.'

I had no words, just stared at her. I was too shattered by the labour and the birth to summon up the energy to be really scared. As she left, my last conscious thought was that even if my baby died, there was no way I could ever contemplate going through again the horrors that I had just experienced, or putting another baby through what Cara had just gone through. Guilt washed over me and then, incredibly, I fell asleep and slept without dreaming or without any disturbance for the next eight hours.

David was beside my bed when I finally woke up properly. He had already awoken by himself, suddenly seized with the intuition that something was very wrong, just before the telephone rang to summon him back to the hospital.

We were told that Cara had restarted breathing by herself and that she seemed to be fine. We were torn between wanting to believe this and being terrified that she would do it again; I was especially anxious, because I had not noticed the first time. The paediatrician told us that they were working on the assumption that she had contracted an infection during delivery and were going to treat her with antibiotics.

When I look back on that week, all I seem to remember is putting as brave a face as I could on a catalogue of really upsetting events. I remember Cara with a black eye, a bruised and swollen arm, and a deep cut on her forehead (which left a permanent scar), crying because of the pain. I remember the paediatrician trying to put a drip into her arm and failing to find a vein because she had so much body fat, and her screams of pain, and dissolving into tears myself because handing your child over to a doctor who is going to hurt her is against every maternal instinct. I remember her being badly jaundiced and knocking the top off her light box with flailing arms.

All I wanted to do was to grab my baby and run away. My mind, feverish and hormonal, dwelt crazily on extreme and impossible horrors. The whole experience was so terrible that for about two months afterwards, I was unable to talk about it.

But finally, the day came when Cara and I were released from hospital. I was better at home, though still very sore. People came to see us; my mother stayed with us to help for the first month. Cara fed well and appeared normal, but I still felt very inadequate and somehow as though I always got it wrong when I tried to follow my instincts with her. Even then, there was a withheld quality about her that baffled me. I would look into her beautiful dark-blue eyes, fringed with thick, long dark lashes, and see not a child who looked back at me, but an enigma. I would think that I knew her and then be surprised all over again when I didn't know what she wanted. But I loved her desperately and believed what I had been told, that the apnoea episode (when she had stopped breathing temporarily in her sleep) had been the result of her traumatic birth. No fewer than five paediatricians had told us this at the hospital and who were we to disagree?

Gradually, we slipped into a routine: little outings in the car, feeding, bathing, changing, feeling contented that we had achieved parenthood at last. For three months we lived in the soft cocoon that all new parents experience, when life revolves around the baby and everyone is generous and kind. We began to plan her christening and I started to embroider a cross-stitch sampler for her. Those days are especially poignant in the light of what was to follow.

It was David, who had never really believed that the apnoea episode was without significance, who first noticed that there seemed to be something wrong with Cara's eyes. She seemed to glimpse a toy almost by accident, follow it for a short while and then drift away. She also seemed to have a squint that persisted long after it should have resolved itself. Although content to be held, she did not seem to actively enjoy cuddles and would pull her hands away when they were taken. It was all very subtle: nothing definite, just a series of little things. But she was gaining weight, and apart from bad colic in her first few weeks, everything seemed to be well with her. She had passed her six-week check without any major problem being identified.

But gradually, the milestones started to be unusually late: the first roll, the first active grasping for a toy. And her eyes didn't improve; instead, they either appeared sleepy and unfocused, or else they gazed upwards. Our health visitor referred her to the orthoptist, who referred her to the Eye Infirmary, who in turn could find nothing obviously wrong with her eye structure and referred her again to a neonatal neurologist at Sunderland Royal.

I cannot believe how innocent we were as the date of the appointment approached in June 1998. We should have known that no appointment of this kind was made without a significant problem having been spotted, but we convinced ourselves that it would be all right, and that after that particular Friday, we would just get on with the preparations for the christening, which was to take place on the Sunday of the following week.

We arrived at the hospital in the afternoon and found our way to the neonatal medicine building. After a short wait, we were ushered in to see the neurologist, a bearded, weary-looking man in a muddy-coloured wool sweater. As we talked, his hands examined Cara, whom he held on his lap. She was wearing a white romper suit, printed with pink bows, because it was a hot day. He undressed her, looking at her eyes, her arm movements, her head and neck. Finally, he spoke.

'I think she is fitting,' he said quietly. 'The way her arms are flying up – that is not a normal movement, and it could indicate a seizure, possibly many seizures. I'd like to do a short EEG here, but I would also like to refer her to the General Hospital in Newcastle for further investigations. She does seem to have an unusual degree of head lag too, see?' And he held Cara's little arms to pull her up. Her neat little head lolled back lifelessly.

'Oh no, no!' I cried, willing him to tell me he had got it wrong. 'Please, she's so small and I love her so much, please . . . ' My voice tailed off into tears as I knew that it was hopeless and that this man's words which had shattered our small, peaceful world would haunt me for ever. This was something for which I had been completely unprepared. A new future loomed on the horizon, one full of huge and horrible possibilities, one that no parent wants for his or her child. David asked him some questions as he prepared to take Cara away, but I was crying so much that I couldn't hear what they were. She was being taken from me again, back into the hands of the doctors, no longer exclusively ours because this thing that was wrong with her made more intrusions necessary and meant that others would have to be admitted, whoever they were, because they knew more about our child than we did. And it would be a pattern, for good and ill, for the rest of Cara's life.

We called my mother to let her know what was happening. The EEG test on the electrical activity of Cara's brain seemed to indicate that she was indeed fitting, so she was immediately put on the appropriate anticonvulsant, carbamazepine, and admitted to Sunderland pending transfer to Newcastle General on Monday. Stunned, we managed to get through the weekend and postponed the christening for another month, hoping against hope that everything would be all right.

The following Monday, Cara was duly transferred. The first day of tests happened, then the second, and turned up nothing. We were installed on a ward with horrible Victorian tiles in the rooms, grim, despite attempts to make it look better with pictures; a ward that specialized in neurological conditions in children, conditions that we learned later were often fatal. We waited and waited. One incident sticks in my mind as all of this was going on, outweighing all the kindness of the nursing staff. One of the junior consultants came back with Cara to the room and said, almost as a challenge, 'Well, we've tested for all the usual things and now we're going to look at the others, and you'd better hope it's none of those, because they're all very serious.' She peered through her black-rimmed glasses at me as I cried and then, seeming to be satisfied that she had done her bit for medical science, whisked out through the door again, leaving my poor mother to try to pick up the pieces and comfort me as best she could.

There had been no need to tell me anything at all at that stage. It may have been a misguided and tactless desire to inform, but at the time, it felt more like gratuitous cruelty. I think it probably coloured every subsequent encounter I ever had with a medical person about Cara. To the day of Cara's death, I remained terrified of doctors who seemed to put the fact that she was an interesting case before the fact that she was a child who was part of a family, and I never got used to hearing her problems described in a detached, scientific way that at times seemed to verge on relish.

The third day came, and Cara was anaesthetized so that an MRI scan could be performed to check for abnormalities in the physical construction of her brain. She lay in my mother's arms afterwards, whimpering in her sleep because the fluid that had been injected had given her a headache. For me it was a continuation of the emotional pain I had suffered at her birth, another reminder of my helplessness and inability to make things better for her.

Finally, the senior neurologist came to see us, accompanied by the woman I had encountered before, who this time, mercifully, stayed quiet.

He broke the news hurriedly, trying to get it over with quickly. Cara's brain was several millimetres too small for the size of her skull, enough to give her a global developmental problem that could be very serious or fairly minor – no-one could tell. It did not look as if it had been the result of brain damage but rather of lack of development, and he had no idea what could have caused it. It did not have a name and it conformed to no known syndrome. About 5,000 children were born every year with it and it did not appear to correlate with the age of the mother. Cara's ability to process visual information was impaired, not because there was anything wrong with her eyes, but because her brain had a very limited capacity to understand what was being seen; that was why her eyes did not appear to be working: functionally, she was very close to blindness.

As I was sobbing, I heard David ask what the treatment was.

'There is no treatment at present. I'm sorry. We can only monitor her. Do you want to see the scans?' he asked, obviously uncomfortable and keen to leave us.

David went with him. My mother stared down at her only grandchild, still sleeping restlessly in her arms with a plaster on the side of her head. I had stopped crying and was looking in disbelief at the shreds of our life. I felt then, and for many years afterwards, as though the doctor had taken an axe and split me right down the middle, from the top of my head to my navel. Cara was the one with the brain injury, but the diagnosis was one that devastated the whole family. For the rest of her life, we carried those scars and shared in her lack of wholeness, because the pain never left us. As her mother, I never stopped grieving.

'Would you like a cup of tea?' asked the nurse, pleasantly.

I didn't look at her, but I spoke very deliberately. 'No thank you, I wouldn't.'

My mother nodded, and the nurse left the room. I left too. I heard my mother calling after me, but I was suddenly desperate to get out. I got on a bus and went into town. I travelled to Jesmond, ending up in the building leased by the Samaritans, after I had scraped my arm along a wall to make it bleed to give vent to the rage I felt.

I can't remember who I spoke to, only that it was a woman and that she managed to calm me down sufficiently for me to go back to the hospital, about an hour and a half later. By this time, David had been about to call the police and was yelling at the hospital staff for leaving me alone. I submitted to having my arm dressed and to being questioned by a psychiatrist, who pronounced me sane, but in shock.

I was not coping and I didn't cope for several weeks afterwards. David went to see Cara, but I was so terrified of what she might do that I couldn't. My confidence as a mother was non-existent and I was desperately afraid that some little mannerism that I had previously found cute and endearing would turn out to be the sign of something sinister. I was overwhelmed then with a sense that I could not look after her, and the future was a black hole that I couldn't even contemplate. All my feelings of inadequacy as a mother, everything that I had experienced that had whispered to me that I did not know her, that she was not quite like other children, opened up and paralysed me, because now other people were telling me the same thing. I adored her, but the grief that was part of that emotion disabled any capacity I might have had to take care of her. Then I became angry, but not with her, only with the over-whelming helplessness and with the medical world because we lived in the twentieth century and still couldn't treat this kind of problem.

When I recovered, it became much more important for me to cope and be strong than to show any sentiment. I had to survive in order to look after her. Thereafter, my emotions, except with close family, went inward. Outwardly, over time, I developed an efficient, coping persona that hid my pain from most of the world but also gave me a reputation with some people of extreme reserve, which later on did not always work in our favour.

David, in the meantime, was suffering his own process of adjustment. He told me afterwards that the first neurologist we had seen had told him that we would now have to make a decision about having Cara adopted, since many families in our situation often broke up because of the pressures. Perhaps it was true, but it was not what David needed to hear at the time.

I went to my family doctor asking for medication, but was told that I would have to manage by myself, apart from some very low-dose sleeping tablets, which he gave me after a lot of arguing. I imagine he was trying to stop me becoming addicted, but I found his stance unhelpful and not typical of other doctors I had encountered. When I said that I didn't think I could cope if the baby came home, I was told shortly that I would have to and that legalities would be invoked if I did not.

It seemed that only one doctor, a junior paediatrician, empathized with our situation and allowed us to talk, without passing judgment or telling us what we should do. When I look back, we could have done with a lot more of that approach, but we didn't get it. It felt as though everybody was scattering about trying to get things tied up and off their hands; even the consultant obstetrician in charge of my case rang up to find out what was going on. I guess that she suspected that the damage had been caused by the birth. The bomb had gone off, there were pieces flying about everywhere, and everyone was running for cover.

Of course, things did begin to settle down, at least on the surface. Some counselling was arranged for me. It helped a little, but not much: the people I saw had no experience of the devastation I was going through, and as it was an ongoing trauma it couldn't be resolved, no matter how much I talked about it. I couldn't 'move on' because I had to confront the situation day after day. I needed only practical support with childcare and a chance to get used to what couldn't be altered. Information about what to expect might have been useful, but no-one could give us any because no-one could give us a detailed prognosis.

I don't really know how we survived in those weeks and months just after the diagnosis, except that we didn't talk a lot about it if we could help it. David escaped into computer games; I tried to escape into reading, television and occasionally, when I felt very bad, into one too many glasses of wine (a habit which I soon stopped because it made me feel too ill).

Curiously enough, the only television programme that made me forget what was going on in my life was *Changing Rooms*, which was new at the time. For half an hour, I sat watching Linda Barker or Laurence Llewelyn-Bowen transforming houses, sometimes dreadfully, sometimes wonderfully well, and I could leave my life behind. Laurence Llewelyn-Bowen has commented that changing your sheets and colour schemes may make you feel good but won't improve your marriage or make you more successful. But watching that programme helped me to survive one of the most difficult times of my whole life. Looking back, perhaps I was subconsciously acting out my desperate need for transformation. As soon as I was fit enough, I started painting our new-build house (which had had mostly 'magnolia' walls for nearly four years), using different colours and trying out paint effects. To this day, if I am stressed, I get out the paintbrush and perform another transformation ritual.

We were given a list of childminders, because I would soon be going back to work: the minder would have Cara for two days a week and my mother agreed to take Cara for one day. David would work from home on Thursdays and Fridays so that I did not have to cope on my own. Although nothing would ever be normal again, a routine was established that helped me to lose some of my extreme insecurity. Working helped in the short term, but I feared being regarded as a weak link, as people with 'baggage' often were, so I gave up in November, never to return.

A traumatic year ended with Cara catching bronchiolitis (a lung infection common in small babies) the week before Christmas, only being released from hospital, thin and pale, on Christmas Eve. Determined something was going to go right, I grimly cooked Christmas dinner for us all.

## 3 Fear and Hope

The explosion that had wrecked our old life had settled, but nothing could ever be the same. We now had a child, but we couldn't really mix with other people who also had children because their children were all right and it was too painful to have to explain why Cara couldn't do things. She remained beautiful to look at and physically totally normal in most of her appearance, so it wasn't at that stage obvious that she had a serious problem.

I continued to escape into books, sitting up in bed at night rereading old favourites. One of these was *Nicholas and Alexandra* by Robert K. Massie. He is himself the father of a haemophiliac son and he attributes many of the mistakes made by Tsar Nicholas and his wife to the fact that they were dealing with the terrible uncertainty of their son Alexei's haemophilia. I identified very much with the tsarina, who withdrew into her private world in order to be able to deal with the anxiety and grief over her child's illness, and I understood her much better in the light of what we were going through, both individually and as a couple.

I was raised in the Methodist Church, the third-generation recipient of a 'respectable', working-class subculture that taught personal responsibility and social action. Growing up during the 1960s, we heard a lot about Martin Luther King in church, about the importance of not necessarily accepting the views of the majority if these led to injustice for other people. I was brought up to be serious and responsible about how I lived my life and was told many times over, at home and at church, that to swim against the tide was often the only thing to do, but not necessarily something that would bring popularity.

Not surprisingly, I was a shy, over-serious child and teenager who often felt conflicted between my rebellious side and my rather haphazardly developing nonconformist conscience. I loved clothes, make-up and good times, but I could when it suited me be utterly uncompromising on what I saw as points of principle, for example, on bullying, which I always hated and spoke out against. I was an only child in a family that consisted largely of adults and I was the first on my mother's side to go on to higher education. There was enormous affection, but there was also a burden of high expectation. In the church the sense of community was excellent in those days, but the personal love and passion for God that had motivated Wesley and his contemporaries were largely missing. My family were good churchgoers but disliked evangelistic sermons, finding them old-fashioned and undignified.

When I was seventeen, I failed spectacularly in my first attempt at my A level exams, and for the very first time in my life, I realized that my path might not be as untroubled as I had always believed. Because I was a thoughtful teenager, that realization led on to thoughts about my life in general: what was it about, what were the important things, did I matter at all? How was I to beat the fear of failure that constantly sat on my shoulder now and threatened to paralyse me in exam situations? 'God, help me. Don't let my life be for nothing.'

The result of all those musings led, perhaps inevitably, back to Christianity; I returned to school for a year to resit my A levels and entered a sixth form in which lots of my contemporaries were asking the same questions at the same time. It was 1978, the year when David Watson brought a Celebrate the Faith team to Newcastle, which presented Christianity as if it was intellectually and emotionally satisfying. It gradually began to resonate with me. I didn't have a Damascus Road conversion, but whereas at the beginning of the school year I wasn't really a committed Christian, by the time I had finished my exams in July, I was. Of course, I had very little idea of what that really meant or of what to do next.

I entered Newcastle University in October with a sheaf of good results but was confused by the different kinds of Christianity on offer. I liked the commitment to good personal behaviour shown by the evangelicals in the Christian Union but found their sometimes over-enthusiastic approach to evangelism scary. I liked my liberal friends but found their faith too impersonal and too conveniently flexible. I enjoyed my periodic trips to the Catholic chaplaincy, whose members definitely gave the best parties, but they belonged to a culture that was very different from my own roots. The charismatics, whom I discovered properly in my third year, seemed to be the kindest and the most personally committed, but I found their worship marathons a bit overwhelming and their theology hard to evaluate properly when hyped up with all that emotion.

So I never really found a church 'home', probably because I wasn't confident enough, among all these unwaveringly certain Christians, in my own identity. I became a teacher, following the completion of an English degree, but I hated it and left the profession after a couple of years. I got involved with a charismatic group that became a house church but had some bad experiences and left. And I married, briefly and disastrously, when I was twenty-seven: by the time I was thirty, I was divorced, solvent, retrained and working as a librarian but my life had fallen short of its early promise by a long way, and although I hadn't lost my faith, I knew that it needed a drastic re-evaluation.

I needed to find out who I was and exactly what I did believe before I was able to integrate all the stuff about God. Because my conversion had been so gradual and so obviously real, I never questioned the truth of the faith, only of my own understanding of it. So I read and thought and made new friends and lived my life and attended my local parish church, listening to the liturgy, soaking up a form of Christianity that was there without demanding an immediate response from me in return.

It was during this period in my life that I met David, who at the time was a cheerful agnostic/theist but who was so obviously destined to become part of my life that our marriage was inevitable and a real gift for both of us.

Into this situation came our first child, needy beyond imagining. When the initial shock had subsided, I sat at home and thought and thought. And gradually I got beyond the immediate and pressing worries about Cara and I began to wonder how this all fitted into the context of the faith that I still followed. Could God do something to help my daughter and us? Would he? How should I approach Cara's situation from a faith point of view, since the vast resources of modern medicine could do so little for us?

David's response was to throw himself into work as much as possible and to start to think about a trust fund for Cara; instead of being his relaxed, effortlessly successful self, he became driven to a degree that was even noticed by some of his colleagues. My response was to adopt survival strategies and to live from day to day with the pain or with a distraction from it.

We were pretty well left alone by the medical and support services to begin with. We changed our consultant; our new specialist was Dr Bamra, the elegant, poised head of the Child Development Unit at Sunderland, who spoke in a soft, heavily accented voice, wore immaculate clothes and was less clinical in her approach than those doctors we had previously encountered.

Cara was given an allocation of half an hour of physiotherapy each week. This was mostly theoretical, because often her therapist would be called away to meetings. I was shown how to do the exercises and I did them every day, without any noticeable results. We were given a series of sensory packs at our request from the Visual Impairment Service, which consisted of materials of different textures and a cassette with different kinds of music, to be used together. I had some hope when I started using these, but there was no response from Cara. It was very hard day after day to work with her when nothing appeared to be changing, but I did it.

Cara was at this time like a perfect little doll; except for an alternating squint, she was a most appealing baby, but she had no connection with the world around her except very fleetingly, and she did not really respond to any kind of stimulus. She began to get ill as she approached her first birthday. I know now that lack of exercise (and she was at this time virtually immobile) results in poor lung function and poor oxygenation that automatically makes the body more vulnerable to viruses and bacteria.

One afternoon, I was working with Cara's sensory pack when she suddenly cried out, stiffened and stared without blinking for several minutes. Her face went very pale and I knew, even though I had never seen a seizure, that this was what was happening. I frantically telephoned the doctors' surgery, and one of the doctors came out to the house. Fortified by decades of dealing with nervous mothers, he was determined to put my mind at rest.

'She's fine, pet, there's nothing wrong. No seizure, nothing. Yes, I know she's disabled, but you have nothing to worry about here, really.'

I wasn't convinced, but I wanted to believe him, so I filed the episode away, as I had so many other things, in the 'think about it another day' category.

Cara caught a throat infection that spring, but although she was miserable, nothing else too untoward happened. However, one evening after she appeared to have recovered, we put her to bed in her room. About half an hour later, there was an unearthly scream; we dashed upstairs to find Cara in a grand mal seizure. Her arms were flailing, her body was twitching and her mouth was moving like a video on fast-forward. While David telephoned for the ambulance, I stayed with her, talking to her, gibbering prayers, trying my utmost to make her come out of it.

The ambulance arrived quickly and we went to the hospital with her. Had we only known it, this would become a well-travelled road for us over the following years. The doctors diagnosed a urinary tract infection and told us that Cara had had a febrile seizure. It was unlikely to happen again, and if we knew she wasn't well, we had to treat her immediately with paracetamol and keep her cool.

Good advice. But as so often with Cara, they were wrong. Although the General Hospital had told us that there was no reason to assume that Cara was epileptic, she did turn out to be epileptic after all. There was much debate about it, because, I imagine, doctors are unwilling to label a toddler. But it became apparent that the seizures were not just caused by high temperatures, though these made the seizures more likely. She was also having 'myoclonic jerks', sudden startles with up-flung arms, in response to loud noises or sudden movements in front of her.

Cara's health thereafter seemed to get worse and worse. She caught chickenpox just after her first birthday and then just seemed to catch endless colds and tummy bugs. With each one, there was now the ever-present threat of seizure. More anguish for us, and still nothing, apparently, that we could do to help the situation.

Since then, I have met many parents who live their whole lives with their disabled children in this way, not asking for or expecting anything more from the system than it already offers. There are others who want more but don't know how to get it, or who are for whatever reason willing to make an uneasy truce and get on with things as they are, even if they aren't especially happy about it. But we somehow just couldn't do that. Driven by our need and unable to stand back and watch our child suffer, we finally turned from victims into fighters.

I could cope with Cara's disability a day at a time; at the very least, it was predictable. But I could not watch her health suffer, and in particular I could not stay at home with her – sleep nights in the house with her – with the ever-present possibility of seizures looming over our heads, so that we were never safe from the fear of going into her room one morning and finding that she had died in the night. Whatever it was, there had to be more than what was currently on offer: the limited therapy, the information vacuum, the unwilling-ness to do more than offer palliative help because research into brain injury in children, we were told by the doctors we asked, was seen as a low priority. Even worse than that was what appeared to be the general assumption that Cara just wasn't going to get any better and that our entire function as parents was to 'take her home and love her', an approach that infuriated us, because how would it be possible when we were unable to manage her disability effectively?

I began to feel that Cara's uncertain diagnosis might be a good thing. It allowed us to hope. There was just a faint possibility that she might turn out to be OK – well, OK-ish – though at present the signs weren't very good. Although I am naturally a fairly pessimistic person, no-one can or should build their lives on despair. Hope is a major survival instinct, hard-wired into the human personality. Christianity traditionally calls it a virtue that should be cultivated, in the light of the general hope that we have in Christ, but I hadn't heard much preached about it.

I found a lot more within Judaism, an important thread in my understanding of my own faith, about the importance of hope in adversity, its maintenance, its cultivation, its celebration. A story that I found in one of Adrian Plass's books meant a great deal to me at this time. It was told to him by the late rabbi, Hugo Gryn, about the time that he spent in Auschwitz as a teenager with his father. The festival of Hanukkah falls in December and celebrates the deliverance of the temple from the enemy, and the oil that miraculously lasted for eight days so that the temple could be purified and rededicated. As Hanukkah approached for the inhabitants of their wooden hut, Hugo's father began to hoard part of his daily ration of margarine and asked him to do the same, because they were going to celebrate Hanukkah in the traditional way, with nine lights. When Hugo protested and asked why they were wasting rations that might help to keep them alive, his father replied that, while humans could live for a long time without food, and even for a while without water, no-one could last for one minute without hope. So they had their ceremony, the lamp-wicks made of blanket threads, some Polish Catholics and a Lutheran minister celebrating with them.

Gryn noted in his autobiography that the lamps guttered and went out very quickly, but they had served their purpose. For them, the lamps represented variously their hope for survival, for more just times, for a civilized and dignified life again, and were an acknowledgment that even here, God was present, and they were still in his heart, as his chosen ones, his covenant people.

I began to pray. If I was going to do anything at all to help Cara, my own mindset had to be right and I had to start looking at what I actually believed about all of these questions: suffering, answered prayer, the possibility of miracles.

I happened to switch on the television one morning, and while channel-flicking, encountered the God Channel. I began to be drawn into it as I sat on the sofa, Cara in her little seat asleep beside me. I began to watch it every day and I particularly liked Joyce Meyer's programme, *Life in the Word*. Her humour and her pithy observations, delivered in her down-home, gravel-toned voice, were like a forceful finger prodding me and telling me not to give way to the emotions that swirled around inside me but to trust in God for my deliverance. 'Straighten up and fly right!' It was a bit like being addressed by Aunt Eller in the musical *Oklahoma*.

Above all, the whole channel was about a positive, upbeat faith that refused to be limited by circumstances. It was tough-talking, it could be simplistic, it could even be a bit tasteless; like the widow pestering the corrupt judge in Jesus' parable (Luke 18:1–7), it encouraged a direct, even pushy approach to prayer, but it was an approach that I badly needed at the time and that I am deeply grateful for. It enabled me to connect with my emotions and offer them to God as they really were, in expectation that he would act and that I should be ready. I know of no better way to approach a situation like ours.

I believe that suffering is part of our life in Christ, but it isn't the whole of that life and it shouldn't be made an excuse for morbidity and apathy. I have been a lifelong Eeyore, with until then a bias towards believing the worst scenario, but living with Cara changed me into a cautious, though rather insecure, optimist – simply because it was the only thing that helped me to survive.

In the months after Cara's diagnosis, I read the book of Job, not really understanding very much of it except to draw the conclusion that sometimes there aren't 'answers' to the problem of pain in any easy, concrete sense. A book that helped at lot was David Watson's *Fear No Evil*, written with tremendous courage as he faced the probability of his own death through bowel cancer. The part of it that really sticks in my mind is that the correct response to suffering is not really 'why', but 'what' and 'how': what is God saying to me in this and how do I line myself up with what is going on so that the best possible outcome is achieved?

I returned to reading Susan Howatch's *Starbridge* novels and began to understand the context in which our catastrophe had happened. She depicts a fallen, imperfect and unpredictable world where bad things happen to both guilty and innocent people seemingly without differentiation; in most cases, we do not bring these calamities on ourselves, but we still have to live with them. However, it is a world that because of Jesus is still in the process of redemption, being re-created, still held in God's love and destined in the end for complete perfection. And the best thing we can do is to become part of the dynamic personally, seeking to be involved in the solution rather than part of the problem. As we were to discover, this brings its own challenges and pitfalls, but on the whole is a much better option than sitting scraping one's sores on the rubbish heap.

So the information went in and enabled me to get a handle on what was going on. My days with Cara settled into a routine, and prayer became interwoven with everything. The scripture that I held in my head at this time was,

Be strong and let your heart take courage,
all you who wait for, and hope for, and expect the Lord!
(Psalm 31:24 Amplified Bible)

given an individualized therapy programme, consisting of physiotherapy and intelligence exercises that were done each day, by families and teams of helpers.

I think the point about the book that drew us in the most was Doman's assertion that 'Parents are not the problem with children. Parents are the answer',[1] because by that time we were so utterly fed up with being treated like halfwits by many of the professionals we saw when we tried to contribute anything to the understanding of Cara's problems. We knew nothing much about conductive education (pioneered at the Peto Institute in Hungary and used extensively with cerebral-palsied children) but in any case, at that time it was not thought suitable for children with Cara's level of disability. A similar method of education through repeated exercises and tasks was Bobath therapy, but we only heard of this much later.

The part of the book that really gripped me, however, was the part that described a method of treating epilepsy without the use of drugs. Over a period of time, a specially constructed mask was placed over the nose and mouth for one minute only, at no less than five-minute intervals. The purpose of this was to encourage the child to breathe an increased amount of carbon dioxide; as a result, a number of benefits emerged: the child's chest capacity improved, leading to a reduction in respiratory infections and better circulation, and the habit of breathing deeply seemed to reduce the frequency and severity of seizures, in some cases even allowing medication to be discontinued altogether. It had always been Cara's seizures that had scared me the most and now, it seemed, here was the beginning of a solution.

I can still recall the excitement with which I hurried in to the Children's Centre to talk to Cara's consultant. I did not want us to be operating outside NHS expertise and I did not want to undertake any form of treatment that was potentially harmful, but I really wanted to try this. She listened calmly and said, yes, it was fine with her if we wanted to do it.

Because we were unaware of any centre in the UK that did Doman-Delacato therapy, we began to think about emigration to the States; David had already been offered the possibility of a job in North Carolina when he had worked there at the beginning of the year. The only difficulty might be medical insurance for Cara, which could turn out to be prohibitively high. Then there was the option of visiting the Institutes in Philadelphia, but we could probably not afford to fly there regularly as the therapy required us to do. Then came the solution, right out of the blue.

My mother had been leafing through a magazine when she had come across an advert for a certain centre in Somerset. The wording was almost exactly the same as that on the book we had read, so we duly ordered the book that explained the story of the centre, written by the founder, Keith Pennock. I telephoned one Saturday morning, expressed a desire to go – and that was it. We booked a bed and breakfast and set off on the long drive to Somerset, filled with hope and believing we had begun to find a solution to Cara's difficulties.

# 4 The Alison Centre, Changes and Challenges

It was a Sunday evening when we parked our car outside the farmhouse where we were staying, with a bit of early spring rain falling. The thing I recall most about the farmhouse is that the landlady was growing hyacinths in bowls indoors and the smell pervaded some parts of the house to a point where it was almost overpowering.

The following morning we pulled up to the Alison Centre itself, an old house with a wheelchair ramp built on the back. We met the Pennocks, who ran the centre; there was Keith, a vigorous, confident man in his sixties, with lively blue eyes and a big white beard; his wife Val, a former physiotherapist with untidily curling hair and a gentle voice and manner; and one of their daughters, Judy, young and very slim, with ethnic bracelets around her thin, tanned wrists.

It was Val who went through the initial questionnaire with us: a good couple of hours of careful data collection that concentrated on our view of Cara and her abilities and difficulties. We then spoke at length to Keith about Cara's history and our history as a family, and he was sympathetic and very positive.

We had read his book, so I knew their story. Alison, their eldest daughter, had become badly brain-injured after an allergic reaction to the rubella vaccine and they had taken her to the Institutes in the States. As a result of the Doman-Delacato programme, she had not only survived life-threatening seizures but had grown up to have a much better quality of life than anyone had predicted for her. Although Keith never promised us a miracle, it helped a great deal to have someone who had been through the same as us speaking encouragement and feeding our need to hope and to act positively. It was a bit like meeting Churchill when you had been used to listening to Neville Chamberlain: bracing, encouraging, slightly maverick, with enormous force of will and personality.

In the afternoon, Cara was given a physical assessment according to the programmes she would be following and then we were sent home early with instructions to arrive back for 9.30 am the next day. The rest of the week was very busy: lectures for an hour in the morning, then working on Cara's programmes until about 3.30 pm, when we would finally retreat to go somewhere and regroup.

We did a lot of exploring during that particular week. I had visited Glastonbury before but had not felt quite so aware of its 'alternative' culture. On the main street, there were all manner of therapies to be had, or practices to try: aura reading, psychic healing, Tarot cards, yoga – it was bound to be there. The town was like a 'spaghetti junction' of the New Age, with different paths leading everywhere and anywhere. Given our circumstances, it might have been expected that we would want to pursue some of them, but David, who was then not a committed Christian, found them too scary and I, who was, knew that however desperate I was, such paths were definitely not for me.

We were given advice at the centre about diet for Cara. We had always tried to feed her well, but we were told that too much salt or sugar is especially bad for children who are prone to seizures.

The masking treatment I had no problems with. I think we both held our breath when we tried it out for the first time with Cara at the centre, but she did not seem to be unduly upset by it and we were very careful to stick strictly to the protocols. We were given Cara's programme, which was to be undertaken with the aid of volunteers whom we would have to find, but we could begin to do some of it. During four sessions with her throughout the day, I would be doing the masking, the sensory stimulation, the homemade flashcards, and certain physiotherapy exercises that were prescribed, with her main physiotherapy session in the evenings.

We came home and began to set up our equipment and to try to find our volunteers. We created a notice that we distributed to three churches giving details of what we were doing, a beautiful picture of Cara, and our phone number; the response was amazing. I suppose it was inevitable: many churches are full of retired people who may not see their grandchildren very often and who would love to feel useful and to spend time with a small child again on a regular basis. I filled a whole address book with people's names and phone numbers, sorted out their available evenings and set up a rota. At the beginning, we had about two dozen volunteers; although this fell off a little towards the end, we always had some people, and they were incredibly good about regular attendance and punctuality.

As the programme became established, we drew others in. It was wonderful for Cara to have so much attention and she loved it, becoming a happy, giggly toddler who was able to recognize and respond to some people and who thereafter always seemed to love being in company. I know how big an impact she made on the lives of many of those who were involved with us and I think that this was probably the best period of her life, because she was given unstinting love and attention by everyone. All who were involved with this part of Cara's life deserve our highest praise and thanks for everything they did, even if, in the end, it didn't have the effect we were all hoping for.

So there I was, coordinating Cara's volunteers, making flashcards, doing her daytime programmes, masking her, cooking her healthy food. But at the same time I also found that I had to justify our choices to some of her NHS therapists, who were at best uninvolved and at worst very sceptical about some of the things we were doing. We were questioned especially about the masking, which was viewed as risky. I had in some way always been a person who questioned the status quo, but I never believed that I knew more about the general picture of Cara's difficulties than the doctors and therapists, even if they didn't always seem terribly helpful when we needed them. I began to feel tired and stressed, and to feel that we were being asked to carry a responsibility that was too much for us.

I felt trapped between the two schools of thought that govern conventional and alternative medicine, systems that sometimes conflict. The thing that both sides seem to have in common is that, at least to the outsider, they are suspicious and sometimes dismissive of the other and avoid dialogue. I understand that doctors are conditioned by their training to be loyal to the system in which they have been trained and are often unwilling to look at other methods, while alternative practitioners may rely too much on their own instincts and on untested treatments developed from limited research.

My desire would be that the medical establishment take more seriously the need for quality of life for brain-injured children; there is little point in saving the life of a severely premature baby if the child is going to be condemned to the half-life experienced by many children with difficulties because no-one is sufficiently interested in trying to make their lives worth living. Such an approach more or less forces committed and aware parents to look elsewhere for help.

I felt it more than David, because he was then preoccupied in keeping everything going financially, and since I had had more experience in the alternative field than he had, he tended to leave more of the decisions about this area to me. I prayed and I trusted, but I worried too.

Then, into this somewhat volatile situation came something that threatened to derail our lives all over again. I was having problems with my teeth, had seen the dentist and had been booked in a few days later for a dental X-ray. As I left the dentist's and went into the nearby chemist's shop, some impulse made me buy a pregnancy-testing kit. The following morning, I duly dipped the tester – and stared in absolute disbelief as a blue line slowly appeared.

It is hard to describe my feelings at this time. On one level, I was absolutely thrilled; on another, I was gripped by the most terrible fear. Since we did not know what had caused Cara's disability, I would be walking on eggshells for the next nine months, afraid to eat this, breathe that, catch something else. Then there were the day-to-day demands of looking after Cara and doing her programme.

All these thoughts were crashing about in my head as, after telling David and my mother, I went to my doctor's appointment.

'I don't want prenatal testing,' I said, 'and I want a Caesarean. I won't go through what happened last time.'

He said something soothing and then I asked about progesterone supplements; I had been given these when in the early stages of pregnancy with Cara by the hospital.

'We wouldn't normally prescribe those,' he said. 'They aren't available on the NHS.'

How I wish I had probed further and asked him to refer me back to the hospital! I now know that I have always had a problem with my progesterone receptors which becomes worse under stress. But at this point, I knew nothing about it, so I blithely carried on with my active life. Yet I was so tense that I sat up into the early hours watching TV because I couldn't sleep. I walked the dog and swam when I could, because exercise had always been a good stress-buster for me, but it didn't work this time. I felt more and more exhausted, and the more tired I was, the more I worried.

It couldn't continue, of course. About eight days later, I started to bleed, and I lost the baby two days after that. As I stared at the fragile little fish that lay, quite dead, in my hand, I felt that I had finally hit rock-bottom. My second child was dead and I might never have another.

Gradually, things returned to normal as I recovered physically, but emotionally, as far as I was concerned, things were never going to be quite the same. Before the pregnancy, my whole life had been just about Cara's needs, but now, although I never felt that she was to blame for the miscarriage, a re-evaluation was going on. I began to question the validity of spending so much of my life doing Cara's programme. We were, even after this short time, already beginning to see good results in terms of her physical health, but there was nothing so far to indicate that it was helping to develop her cognitive abilities or her movement.

I allowed myself to think ahead. Keith Pennock's book had addressed this question, and with typical robustness, he had said, 'First fix the kid. Then have a life.'[1] But what if the kid was unfixable, at least by this method? If we wanted another child, we were going to have to act fast if any medical intervention was needed, and if I did get pregnant again, there would come a point when I would have to stop the strenuous physical work required by the programme.

There was a wider picture to be considered too. I needed other things in my life, because I am naturally inclined to an obsessive approach to problems and challenges, and find it easy to become overstressed. I turned back to my faith as I thought through the issues that had presented themselves as a result of the miscarriage.

My understanding of biblical Christianity, despite the popular image, is that suffering is not meritorious in and for itself. We are not required to seek out suffering for its own sake. Indeed Jesus himself was criticized in his earthly life for having too *good* a time and even he, at the end, said, 'May this cup be taken from me' (Matthew 26:39). Suffering in the Bible is a means to an end, like childbirth, and Jesus' suffering on the cross means that individuals can't earn extra 'points' by acts of personal self-sacrifice. Everyone's life is equally important to God, and everyone has the responsibility to order his or her life towards God in Christ so that it is lived to its maximum potential. This may well involve pain, but it is also supposed to involve joy, challenge, a sense of achievement, and rest and recreation when necessary.

Cara had the right as our daughter to expect that we would do all in our power to help her. We had the responsibility not to run ourselves into the ground by neglecting our own needs. And the child that I lost had had the right to expect that its mother would take proper care of herself. So my conclusion was that our lives should not simply be put on hold for Cara's sake. I would not have survived if I had turned Cara's well-being into my only reason for living. For me, that would have been a form of idolatry and a negation of everything I had learned through my faith.

Slowly, we resumed the programme, but there was less of a sense of being driven, and if I happened to miss out certain things during the daytime sessions, I didn't beat myself up.

The programme did not give us a miracle cure. But without it, we believe that Cara probably would not have survived, given how erratic her health was. That meant that we had precious time with her that we would otherwise have been denied. The best result was that she stopped getting ill and stopped falling prey to every passing virus, with the accompanying seizures. The combination of the masking technique and the regular and rigorous physiotherapy meant that she probably had the equivalent of the exercise a well child of her age would have had while running around and playing.

During her daytime programmes, she would have arm and leg exercises, and techniques to help improve her head lag, and in the evenings, as well as further specific exercises, we also did our 'patterning', an important feature of the programme. We and our two volunteers would move her arms and legs swiftly for five-minute periods to simulate crawling movements. The theory behind this was that the neural pathways would be stimulated and eventually the brain would be able to send the appropriate signals to allow Cara to move for herself. Although this latter was never achieved, as a result of this work Cara developed good musculature and limbs that looked relatively normal with more or less the full range of movement.

Psychologically, it was good for her too. Her generalized 'floppy' hypotonic condition meant that she was always a very laid-back child, but beyond that, she became giggly and much more responsive. The main thing I remember about Cara from this time is her constant laughter, a deep, very adult-sounding chuckle. One of her helpers bought her a hula hoop, covered in sparkly, brightly coloured tape. It was originally intended to help her hand–eye coordination, but it became one of her favourite toys, and when it wore out, we replaced it. She could lie on her back on the floor for hours, turning the hoop up and down, staring at the stripes, in total absorption. After a couple of smacks on the nose, which of course were completely unintentional, our dog learned to give her a wide berth when the hoop came out, and her wrists and forearms became very strong as she practised. The rhythmic *flack-flack* of the hoop, the flash of the colours, and the small brown hands continually moving form one of my strongest memories of Cara, not only at this time but for most of her life.

One day, while I was recuperating from the miscarriage, my mother and I walked the dog and Cara in her buggy up the hill from where we lived, and stumbled on a small estate of self-build houses. One of them was for sale, a tall house that had been designed in an old-fashioned, slightly rustic style. We had been unsettled in our old house for a while for various reasons: we needed more space to do Cara's exercises, David needed more room to work at home, and we both felt that we wanted a bit more privacy.

We first visited the house in August, on a rainy, windy, end-of-summer day. We stepped into a warm, comfortable hallway and then into a living room with a big mahogany fireplace. We waited another month before putting our house on the market and putting in an offer. We sold ours within a fortnight of advertising it and spent the next few months going through the nerve-racking processes of surveys, conveyancing and negotiation over extras, before finally moving in two weeks before Christmas 2000.

We eventually called the house 'Highplace', after a verse from the book of Habbakuk in which the prophet says that, although there may be devastation everywhere, God still enables him to have 'hinds' feet . . . to walk upon [the] high places' (Habakkuk 3:19 Authorized Version). In other words, it is always crucial to look for God's hand in every circumstance and to seek his perspective in order to understand and overcome.

Our lives were changing in other ways too. David, who had always leaned towards some kind of religious belief, was coming to the end of a process of searching that he had started even before Cara was born and diagnosed. The root of my ability to keep going in the circumstances we were currently in was my belief that God was in charge of our lives and Cara's life, and he would show us the way. Naturally, that led me to do lots of reading and thinking, and that spilled over into our conversations, so that David wanted to know more.

At the same time, my own faith was becoming hungrier and more sharply defined. I felt that I didn't really fit in at the church I was attending at the time, which seemed to be increasingly preoccupied with uncertainties and increasingly reticent about issues of belief or personal behaviour. The only way I could cope at that time was to believe simply and directly. Abstract and largely unanswerable questions were about as much use to me then as arguments about the provenance and structure of the lifejacket to a drowning man.

One Easter Sunday, when Cara was in hospital and David had gone in to see her and talk to the doctors, and I was feeling very emotionally ragged, I finally gave in to a growing impulse and visited a local evangelical free church.

It lived up to my expectations. The worship was loud and roof-lifting, without being hysterical, and it was wonderful to again be among a congregation of so many people after years of half-empty churches. The pastor preached in such a clear, unambiguous and relevant way that it was a real refreshment to hear his sermon. As I sat there, I thought, 'This guy's got the goods', and my second thought was, 'I have to get David here to listen to him.'

We began to attend sporadically; David listened, and things began to gel for him at last. When the winter Alpha course began recruiting, he signed up without hesitation; finally provided with the facts and the evidence he needed, at the end of the course he made his decision to become a Christian. Having taken a long time to make his mind up, he is now one of the most steadfast and untroubled believers I know, someone who simply expects God to do his stuff and doesn't worry unduly about the difficult bits.

Cara was welcomed into the Sunday school nursery class, which was extremely good for her. For the first time, she was among able-bodied children, with enough helpers for us not to worry about leaving her there. We joined a house group, and although most of the time I stayed at home to let David go, I did drop in from time to time and got to know people a little.

As we were now active Christians attached to other Christians, I think God decided that we could take a bit of 'course correction', as David calls it. I wouldn't describe this as a disciplinary experience – more of a paring away of extraneous things and a sharper focusing on the important ones.

It began with David's job. The small company that he was working for had decided to split into two companies and he was offered a choice between the two: a difficult decision, because neither was ideal. He chose one on the basis that he would quietly look for other work in his spare time.

About six months into working for the new company, catastrophe struck. David had not been given his P45 form from his previous employers showing his pay and tax details, but from the time he had begun to work for the second company, his taxes had not been paid. He immediately started to pay the taxes back, but we were in straitened circumstances for a while. However, David began to dislike the work and finally decided to go self-employed from home.

This was a precarious existence. Although he had plenty of contacts, the flow of work was erratic. He had taken a more lucrative job on the basis that, if the company had done well, he would have had more than enough money to set up a trust fund for Cara, but he had ended up working harder than ever and with considerably more anxiety. He says that he used to pray every month that he would have enough to pay the bills – and God always delivered. He became very successful but again began to look for a job back in the corporate world, aware that the most important thing for all of us was a level of financial security.

We were also beginning to find that Cara's programme was producing fewer results. I think the Pennocks would have liked us to step it up a bit, but we were already at full stretch and it was starting to be more difficult to find volunteers in our third year. During our January visit, I had a slight spat with Val during a session when we were learning Cara's new programme. It was a sad way to leave the centre. As we pulled away in the car, with snow starting to fall, I felt that something had changed and that there would be more changes in the near future for Cara and us.

Our next visit to the Alison Centre had to be postponed and I was beginning to feel that I didn't want to return to the West Country, where there were so many New Age practitioners. I was by now more aware of the difficulties of the alternative sector and felt that we would do better to get back into the mainstream and start fighting for what Cara needed within it.

As it happened, our next visit, scheduled for November, was cancelled because Keith had to have an operation. Christmas came and went, and we received an email at the end of December from Judy. Keith had died very suddenly after appearing to recover from his surgery, and Val was suspending operations at the centre.

We will never forget Keith, whose unique mixture of bombast and optimism helped to confirm us in our chosen path as hopers and fighters. It certainly wasn't due to any lack of effort on the part of the Alison Centre that Cara failed to improve as much as we hoped. Their contribution and that of our volunteers showed us what could be done if the will was there. Now it was time to go back to the state with everything we had learned, and explore other avenues. We didn't know it at the time, but we were about to enter the longest, hardest and most bitter conflict of all, which would last not only until Cara's death but beyond it.

# Part 2

## Into a Cold War

# 5 Opening Moves

The implementation of legislation is a slow process that in turn creates processes for those who have to be subject to it. It is meant to lay down the rules of 'the game' so that it is played out in an orderly manner and with fairness to both sides; we were to discover that more often the more experienced players are the ones who win because they have much greater knowledge of how it can be played to maximum advantage. Sadly, this is the state of affairs that currently exists between local education authorities (LEAs) and the parents of children with disabilities: an educational machine that assigns to the LEA the presumption of competence and goodwill and makes it very hard for parents who find it to be otherwise.

The Warnock Report, some years before Cara entered education, had promoted the importance of integrating disabled children into mainstream schools. As a result, many local authorities, including our own, had closed special schools and remedial units and had shed professional staff on the basis that auxiliary staff could be taught to do therapies by a reduced number of experts. Although integration was and is a worthy aim, local authorities had often used this objective as a convenient opportunity for cost-cutting, resulting in a greatly diminished service for disabled children and fewer options within special education. At the time when we entered 'the machine', our local authority had had a great deal of practice at trying to fit parents into their own very limited framework, and parents who were interested in their children being educated in a way that was individually appropriate were virtually set up for conflict from the beginning because of the pervasive lack of expertise and resources.

Like the vast majority of parents, however, when Cara's first statement of 'special educational needs' (SEN) was written, we had a very limited idea of all of this and of what our rights were. I don't think we had an unrealistically high view of the system, but at the same time, we were prepared to cooperate with it and to trust what we believed to be the administration of the legal process. However, our views were to become radically different as the result of our experiences.

Cara was a cheerful, healthy three-year-old when we asked for the necessary assessments to take place that would precede her reception into nursery school in 2001. Accordingly, a succession of professionals appeared at our house with clipboards and pens, and as Cara squirmed happily on the floor, we answered their questions as best we could. We had left it as late as we could to have Cara's statement prepared, because we had been told that, as soon as she was identified in a certain way, it would be very difficult to have this changed and we wanted to give her maximum opportunity for improvement. At this time, we were proud of what Cara and we had achieved, and chatted freely about the programmes we had done and their positive effects on her. But there was no answering enthusiasm from any of the professionals we spoke to, and a notable unwillingness to engage in dialogue.

The statement of special educational needs is a key document in the life of a disabled child. It is supposed to be a comprehensive assessment of every aspect of a child's development, identifying every difficulty in a way that is supposed to help teachers arrive at an appropriate educational plan. It is also supposed to specify and quantify the type and amount of therapy that will help the child to improve, including, if necessary, expert advice, and naming a school that the LEA thinks will meet these needs. If it is written correctly and followed by the authority and the school, it drives an effective educational programme that may make a vital difference to a child's progress. If, as seemed to be common among parents we knew, it fails to identify key areas of need and the provision necessary to address them, then it is no use to anyone.

All of this information is now second nature to David and me, but when Cara's first draft statement was produced, we had to learn as we were going along, and it was an intimidating and complex process even for us, who are both university graduates. We can only guess at its effect on people who do not have the confidence to express their views.

We were told that if a child is on the borderline between having severe disabilities, and profound and multiple disabilities, then the general trend is to place her in a school that caters for those less able than she is, rather than more able than she is. We were very clear that we wanted Cara to be in a school for children who were more able, for two main reasons. The first was because of her time in Sunday school, where she had been responsive and happy in the company of well children. The second reason was that we were very afraid of what awaited her if she was placed in a school for children with profound and multiple difficulties. Keith Pennock used to refer witheringly to most such places as 'car parks' – centres where children were deposited for the school day, left in their chairs, cared for, fed, entertained and then returned to their parents.

I visited several schools in the city. The school that we had been recommended to look at in relation to Cara was Coquet Vale, so I looked at it first. From the beginning I had misgivings, because it had then only just come out of 'special measures' after a bad report from the Office of Standards in Education (Ofsted). The 'profound and multiple' children were segregated from the rest of the school in a classroom that was mostly a care centre; the facilities were extremely limited, and when I asked about objectives and targets for individual children, and the amount of time spent out of their chairs, the answers given by the deputy head teacher were negative and evasive. In short, it was a visible embodiment of all the worst things I had been told.

The trouble was that there was hardly anywhere else. Wellington Street took children with behavioural disorders, so I was concerned that Cara would be in physical danger if she went there because she would be unable to get out of the way of any pupil who became violent. The only other school that I could see might be able to help was Plymouth Road which I duly visited, but it was scheduled for merger. The head teacher made a suggestion that was to become the source of our very first battle with the LEA.

'Why don't you try the Sarah Millman School?' she asked. 'They're looking to build up their rolls since a lot of their children have gone into mainstream.'

This school had been scheduled for closure when Cara was still a baby, but the parents and head had put up a spirited fight to keep it open and had succeeded. It had been designated as a school for children with physical disabilities and visual impairment, but since many of these children were now being integrated into mainstream schools, it was widening its net.

I telephoned the school and spoke to the head, who was happy to see me, and when I visited, I was happy with the school. It was a vibrant place; it had good exam results and a national reputation for excellence. The children's work covered the walls, and the pupils we met were confident and well-mannered.

The head was very candid with us; he said that they hadn't previously taken children with Cara's level of disability before, but that he was planning to open a new nursery facility at the school in the old reception class area, and we would be welcome to send Cara there. Whether or not she remained at the school would depend on how well she progressed. We were happy with this decision, although it brought home to us just how precarious Cara's hold on any kind of education might be: if any significant problems arose, she might be back in a 'car park' with the children on whom we believed the education system had given up.

We still had no prognosis for Cara. Naturally, we continued to be full of hope for her and we wanted her to have every possible opportunity. As I look back now, I recognize how discriminatory it is that severely disabled children are given opportunities only if it is considered almost a clear certainty that there will be immediate and tangible results; if well children were educated on that basis, there would be a lot of empty classrooms and unemployed teachers.

So we had our school. What we didn't realize was that the internal politics of the LEA were even then moving in to wreck our fragile plans.

In December, we attended Cara's annual review, at which an employee of the LEA made strenuous efforts to try to get us to accept Coquet Vale, but we were clear that we wanted Sarah Millman for Cara. We came away feeling annoyed, but we were green: we assumed that we would be listened to because we had been told that we had a right to express a preference.

Cara's statement was very late, and finally we started to suspect that something was wrong. In April, David telephoned to find out what was happening, and the official who had been present at the annual review meeting dropped her bombshell: Sarah Millman was now not going to have a nursery class. We could still express a preference, but it didn't really matter, she said cheerfully, because the LEA only 'stuck a pin in a list' anyway. We were upset, but said that we didn't mind as long as Cara did not go to Coquet Vale. When the statement did finally arrive, it named Coquet Vale. The pin had landed in the wrong place.

That was the point at which we started to get angry. It seemed that no-one cared in the slightest what we wanted. We had cared for Cara ourselves with minimal state help all of her life, but it seemed we had no say when it came to where and how she was educated. It seemed that Cara was being shoved into a one-size-fits-all system, which she had been earmarked for even before the statement was written.

After the carefully rationed treatment we had received from the Health Service, we weren't so surprised that Cara could be treated in this way by the LEA. What we weren't used to was the assumption that we would simply accept what they were offering us, or their attitude that they had the right to conceal information from us if it suited them. At this stage, we were not offered a school outside the authority and we were never offered the option of a non-maintained school for Cara, both of which we were entitled to under the Education Act.

At this point, the trust that we had had mostly evaporated and, instead of being our 'partners' as the Education Act had envisaged, the LEA simply became the people that we would have to beat before we could get what we really wanted for Cara: a school that offered some approximation to what we had already tried to do, that respected her as an individual and that would try to help her learn and develop, rather than merely childminding her. No-one would consider this unreasonable for a well child, so why was a severely disabled child seemingly so less important?

When I wasn't being buffeted by anger and frustration, my mind kept dwelling on a phrase from the Scriptures:

> The stone which the builders rejected as worthless
>  turned out to be the most important of all.
> (Psalm 118:22 Good News Bible)

This image can also be found in Isaiah and is quoted by Jesus in relation to himself (see Luke 20:17), but it can also mean anyone who is set aside by human beings but valued by God. The phrase refers to a rabbinic legend that when Solomon's temple was being built, the workmen found an oddly shaped stone that seemed not to fit anywhere, so they put it aside. However, when a cornerstone was required, they looked in vain for an appropriate piece of masonry – and discovered that the one they had dismissed was the perfect shape and size.

It should be an encouragement to oddballs everywhere that God has a place for everyone, but it is particularly important in a social context. Most people would consider that the mark of a civilized democratic society is how it treats its weakest and most helpless members, whether it pushes them to the bottom of the pile or whether it views them through God's eyes, as human beings with dignity and individuality, with potential, however limited, and with the right to be treated as such. In Scripture, the material world of corruption and self-interest is constantly being challenged so that the weakest can receive what is due to them; this is a thread that runs right through both the Old and the New Testaments, and it finds its fullest expression in the life of Jesus, who consciously put himself in the place of the outcast, the unwanted, the inconvenient.

Throughout Cara's life, she too was 'a stone that causes men to stumble' (Isaiah 8:14). For those who wanted to see, she was in every sense a special child, cuddly, pretty, with her tufty honey-blonde hair and big dark eyes that crinkled at the corners when she laughed, who in her vulnerability called out the best that many people had to offer. But she also brought out the worst in many people; there were those who ignored her, who preferred not to spend time with us because of her, and there were many in authority who chose to see her as a problem to be solved in the cheapest way possible.

I had no real doubts that we were pursuing the right course in relation to Cara and that our personal fight for justice for her was part of a much bigger picture. I felt that this fight was a just one and was part of what we ought to do as Christians: ask the difficult questions that challenge those in authority to examine their motives for certain courses of action.

Once, when on a brief holiday in the Cotswolds, I found a Christian bookshop where I bought a wooden plaque. On it was written, 'I know the plans I have for you, plans for good and not for evil, plans to give you hope and a future.' This paraphrase of God's words in Jeremiah was directed towards the Israelites. If he made that promise to those who were capable of choosing to reject him, I thought, then it would certainly apply to Cara, who never had that capability. It seemed to me that it was our job to make sure as far as we could that God's plans for Cara in this world were realized, and that in the absence of any real hope from the doctors or the educators, our hope and faith should be in him, because his will for her was not what the world grudgingly chose to toss in her direction, but something much better.

I did a lot of stamping, swearing and slamming of doors. I am not proud of my reactions but I still believe that we were right to fight. It was an expression of our love for Cara and an inescapable part of our responsibility under God as parents.

I am very glad that I didn't know exactly how difficult it was going to be, for David and me, because I don't know if we would have had the courage to walk into it. I do know that had it not been for our faith, we would have disintegrated many times over. We put so much of ourselves into fighting, only to meet with devastating disappointment, that it would have been entirely reasonable to walk away, and most people would undoubtedly have done so, but we were both stubborn and believed in what we were doing; God himself, I believe, gave us the recovery skills and the will to keep on our chosen path. Psalm 124 begins:

> If the LORD had not been on our side –
>   let Israel say –
> (Psalm 124:1)

The psalm then goes on to describe what would have happened if God had not protected Israel, and that is a fairly accurate summing-up of our lives for the last seven years of Cara's life.

I have been asked if I feel that a more conciliatory attitude on our part would have made things better. It would undoubtedly have made our lives easier, but we believe very firmly that if we had not fought as we did, given the uncompromising attitude of our local authority, Cara would probably not have got even the services that she did get. Her statement was initially written in the vaguest possible terms, which would have placed minimal legal obligations on the LEA, and she would have lost out significantly.

We contacted our local councillor, who tried very hard to help us. She said to us frankly that she did not believe Coquet Vale was the right school for Cara. Cara's paediatrician agreed entirely with us, but by law she was not allowed to name a school. Two of the professionals involved with Cara also said that they felt we had a point; unfortunately, as far as I know, they did not tell this to the LEA, so apart from Cathy (the councillor), we were lone voices. The fight dragged on throughout the year, which in itself, we learned later, was a breach of regulations.[1]

Nothing happened during the summer holidays. At the beginning of the autumn term, we exchanged a few more letters with the authority that were becoming nastier as the situation worsened. At this point, we decided that we needed to seek professional legal advice. The solicitor we saw was reassuring in that he said that unless Cara was proven to be systematically neglected and abused, the authority would be only too happy to save money by leaving her in our care. He also said that we had the right to ask for a home education plan, which would involve the authority sending professionals to our house to provide the service there. The beginning of term came and went without any resolution.

Eventually, Cathy contacted the Under-Secretary of State for Education. By this time it was almost half-term, and a new LEA Director had been appointed who, we heard, was not pleased to get a letter from central government asking her to explain exactly what was going on. Within a few weeks, a solution was proposed: Cara would attend a mainstream nursery, near where we lived, in the afternoons, and would attend Coquet Vale in the mornings. We wrote back saying that we would continue to do Cara's home programme exercises in the mornings, but would be prepared to accept the placement at Broadway Nursery in the afternoons, providing a suitably qualified and experienced helper could be found for Cara.

Cara started her life at nursery in the second half of the autumn term of 2002. Again, it wasn't perfect, because a helper was only available from Wednesday afternoons, so she missed two afternoons at the beginning of her week, but it was a start. Her helper was Annie, a delightful lady with a quietly crazy sense of humour and a liking for Yves St Laurent Champagne perfume, and they got along very well. Although Annie was not a qualified therapist, she was meticulous in doing the prescribed activities with Cara and she helped her fit in with the rest of her classmates. Cara's teacher was also the school's SEN coordinator; her abiding memory of Cara is of her joining in during group story times, drumming her feet on the step of her buggy, giggling and vocalizing.

The children she was with were accepting and helpful. They were too young to have negative attitudes about disabled people; when Cara had her only seizure at nursery, one of the little boys in her class took her hand and talked to her until the ambulance arrived. In general, I think the teachers were surprised by how responsive Cara was, and how much she could do if she was given the appropriate help. They did their very best for Cara, and everyone was sad when her time there came to an end.

At that time, Cara was receiving speech therapy and visual impairment input. But this only happened maybe once or twice every half-term. No physiotherapy was provided, apart from the occasional visit from her assigned physio to 'assess' her (how we came to detest that word!) and give Annie some exercises to do with her, but since we were still doing her programme at the time, that probably had little impact. The low level of professional involvement from the Speech and Visual Impairment departments also meant that they were having very little impact too. However happy we were with the placement at Broadway, we knew that Cara wasn't going to make much progress unless her therapy levels were significantly increased.

When Cara had started at the nursery, we had expected that a qualified helper would be provided for her to cover the days when Annie wasn't available. But the time went on and Cara was still only getting three afternoons instead of five, as her statement specified. She was at this point only four years old, so the provision of educational facilities was more a matter of best endeavours than a legal requirement. In the end, Cara received probably about a quarter of her two-year nursery entitlement and what she did get had only been possible because we had been willing to fight for what we wanted for her. I learned later from a friend who worked as a nursery nurse that this happened quite often with SEN children. Of course, the greater the delays, the smaller the expenditure. Could this have been a disincentive to act quickly in Cara's case?

In the end, this gave us some leverage. Cara had a review at the nursery with the Head of the SEN department, at which we and other professionals involved with her were invited to be present; she had turned five at the beginning of March and we were there to discuss arrangements for her transfer to primary school.

David had been doing his homework. He downloaded a copy of the SEN Code of Practice, a dauntingly wordy and heavy document which outlined the duties and responsibilities of LEAs.

Everyone who was meant to come arrived, and they all sat around congratulating themselves on how well the experiment of putting a severely disabled child into a mainstream nursery had gone. David was genial, jokey and very approachable; I, who had seen him in action many times before, sat back and watched with a carefully neutral expression on my face. After we had listened to everyone's reports, the time came for our contribution.

David pulled out his copy of the Code of Practice and smacked it down on the coffee table like Perry Mason producing a vital witness statement.

'This' – he indicated the code – 'is a really good document. Trouble is, you don't do it, do you?' He grinned in the friendliest way imaginable.

Everyone watched with benevolent interest as he flicked through the pages.

'What this tells me,' he continued, 'is that once Cara turns five, you have to provide what she needs. And you haven't done that, have you? So our proposal is that you immediately find a helper for her to fill the two afternoons at the beginning of the week, and give her a chance at Sarah Millman. If you do that, we won't sue you.' The grin had gone by this time.

The SEN Head's face was a study. It seemed he hadn't realized that he had been subjected to the full Tolchard schmooze from David in order to soften him up for the kill. He looked like a hunter who had suddenly been confronted by a rabbit with a Kalashnikov. He made a gallant recovery.

'Well, er, well, I think you have me there, David. Yes, all right. Obviously Cara has been doing very well here and it seems as if it might be an idea to give her a term at Sarah Millman. OK, we'll draw up the statement along those lines.'

It was our first unequivocal victory, and until then we had lived through so much pain and failure that all the way home we were punching the air and shouting 'Yesss!' like drunken football supporters. We were told that this volte-face by the LEA over the school was a unique occurrence in the memory of those who had attended the meeting. We knew also that once Cara was established in Sarah Millman, resources were so limited that she would probably be there permanently, whatever they said, which is why we had not compromised over Coquet Vale.

It was only afterwards that we realized that we had had to resort to what amounted to legalized blackmail in order to achieve what we wanted. We were beginning to lose our innocence.

# 6 Cara's First School

Cara's first day at school was one of undiluted joy. I dressed her in her blue and grey uniform, lifted her into her buggy and waited without a tear for the taxi to come and pick her up. There was no room for the sentimentality that normally accompanies a child's first departure from home to school, only relief that she was well enough to go and happiness that she was going to the school of our choice.

The school had begun as a charitable foundation and had been awarded an unequivocal 'Excellent' in its last Ofsted report, the only school in Sunderland to be given that designation. However, owing to disagreements between the head teacher and the SEN department, when Cara went there, its new head was there on a temporary secondment from South Tyneside LEA pending the appointment of a new head later in the school year.

In the first week, we were given a timetable for Cara, and a small book to tell us what she had done. Although the timetable was a long way from being as therapy-orientated as we would have liked, we knew that this was the best we were going to get for the moment. The teachers stuck to it very closely, a very important thing for a child like Cara, who needed order and predictability.

Cara enjoyed being at Sarah Millman. She giggled and vocalized on school mornings, responding to the established routine and in anticipation of what was to come, and when she returned at the end of the day, she was also laughing, kicking her heels and waving her arms. The ethos of the school at that time suited her; she was assigned a pupil 'helper' to push her chair and do simple tasks for her, and she gathered around her a group of children who played with her and made much of her.

Had Cara been assigned to the average 'profound and multiple learning difficulties' (PMLD) unit, with its concentration on care rather than on individualized stimulation, I think she would have sunk without trace; here, her personality blossomed and we caught glimpses of the beautiful little girl who lived within the damaged body, and who had responded so well to all the love and care of those who had been involved in helping her. She had invitations to birthday parties and received a raft of cards from the other children at Christmas.

But the uncertainty of her situation was moving in. The acting head told us that she thought that the LEA would be contacting us soon after Christmas about Cara's placement there.

The beginning of the spring term came and went with no ominous brown envelope addressed to 'The Parent or Guardian of Cara Tolchard'; then came half-term, then the end of term with no word. Despite the fact that the SEN Head had had 'concerns' about Cara's placement at Sarah Millman, he had not sought a review at the time he had promised, which had been at the end of the autumn term. The LEA mandarins seemed to have forgotten about Cara. Had events at the school not overtaken her, it is quite possible that she might have been left there indefinitely.

The school had to be given a new designation with the Department for Education and Skills (DfES) as the result of its changing remit, a designation which was supposed to be arrived at as the result of a consultation process between the school governors and the LEA. However, as far as I understand, the LEA began without consultation to push children with autism and Asperger's syndrome into the school, with the long-term objective of turning it into an integrated secondary school/further education college. From our point of view, it meant that Cara's days there were now numbered, since she would not fit the new remit.

Many parents had concerns because they had sent their children to Sarah Millman on the basis that it was a protective, 'special school' environment, and many of them had already tried and failed to make integration work. As well as having a pre-eminent academic reputation, it was the only school in Sunderland that had provided a complete educational environment for special needs children aged five to eighteen years.

This fight was going on in the background while we were waiting for the next confrontation over Cara's education. It came quite unexpectedly at the beginning of May, at her annual review. We turned up on the day, expecting to see the SEN Head and one or two of the therapists who had been involved with Cara. All had sent their apologies, and in the end, there was only the class teacher, the teacher of her proposed class, and the deputy head who was now acting head while the school awaited a new appointment.

We began to try to ascertain how things had gone and what was being done with Cara with regard to therapies provided from outside the school by the Speech and Visual Impairment services. The speech and language therapist had recorded the dates she had visited Cara, but when we checked these we suffered a shock. Cara's class teacher, a gentle young woman with a soft voice, was very clear that the therapist had not been there on some of the dates given.

We asked how the teachers were doing with the visual impairment information included in the statement. They looked at us blankly, with no comprehension. We explained the information as accurately as we could, but no-one seemed to be clear on what we were talking about.

Nonplussed, David moved on to check that Cara was receiving the one-to-one care and assistance that the educational psychologist had recommended. There was no response.

Faced with a deafening silence from the acting head, David finally turned to Cara's class teacher, who had previously given us an honest answer.

'Have you been given Cara's statement?' he asked. 'Has anyone here actually seen it?'

She shook her head. 'I haven't,' she said. 'We were working from her Individual Education Plan.'

'I'm sure it will be here with her records,' fluted the acting head, who was, I think, trying to recover the situation.

David drew our copy out of his bag and proceeded to go through it step by painful step. If no-one there had seen it, then how was Cara's Education Plan drawn up? What about following the procedures laid down in the Code of Practice?

At that point, we accepted that things might have been overlooked. But we were determined to make those present understand that the little help Cara had been allowed in the statement needed to happen, especially the one-to-one help that was necessary for her personal safety.

'Well, you won't get that!' said the acting head emphatically. 'Nobody gets that!'

I raised my eyebrows. So why put it in, if it was never adhered to? Was it really this bad, with vital information being routinely disregarded, even at a school as good as this one?

It was at this time that we first began to explore the possibility of an independent school for Cara. There are no private schools for severely disabled children, but there are some charitable foundations that offer educational opportunities in the same way as private schools do for well children. In our area, we had the Percy Hedley Foundation, a national charity that provides education and residential care for children and adults with difficulties. We looked at Northern Counties School, which was part of the foundation and which took children with severe communication difficulties and complex needs.

When we visited we were very impressed with what we saw, particularly with the number of teachers and specialists employed. We spoke at length to the deputy head, who promised to help us prepare a case for sending Cara there.

'Cara fits our remit,' she said. 'There are certain children who are too complex for the state system to be able to help, who need extra help – special "special needs", if you like.'

We would have to go to tribunal to get Cara there because the LEA would consider the financial outlay to be too much, but we would have a chance. As we left, I wondered fleetingly what it must be like to visit a school where we really wanted Cara to go, a school that really wanted her and where there were no obstacles in the way.

After the review meeting was over, David began to make his telephone calls, first to find out why the SEN Head had not been present. The testy response was that he didn't have the time to attend every annual review. David drew his attention to the fact that the school didn't appear to be adhering very closely to the statement, but as far as the SEN Head was concerned, that was for us to deal with. This was not at all satisfactory, but things drifted on without anything being done and might have continued so, had it not been for one major incident that provoked an almighty response from the LEA. The problem was that it wasn't quite the response we wanted.

By this time, I had finally succeeded in getting pregnant with our second child, at the age of forty-four and after a gruelling journey of fertility treatment. Given my progesterone problem, my gynaecologist was playing safe by prescribing painful injections every three days and I was under strict instructions to rest completely. One Monday towards the end of the summer term, I was trying to relax upstairs when I heard David's key in the door. My mother was downstairs waiting for Cara to come in from school, so I didn't bother to go down. The next thing I knew, David had sat down beside me on the bed and was holding my hand. He spoke very calmly.

'Rhona, Cara has had a slight accident at school. It isn't serious, but they've taken her to hospital just to make sure she's OK and they want me to go and pick her up. It's fine, so don't worry.'

'But what happened?' I asked.

'I don't know the details, but I'll have to go. I'll be back soon.'

David eventually arrived home with Cara about two hours later. He still spoke calmly, because he was trying hard not to upset me, but he was very angry about what had happened.

Cara had been lying on the floor in her classroom with about eight other children, in the care of one teacher. A child in an electric wheelchair had experienced an involuntary spasm and had hit the lever of the chair, propelling her forward. If Cara had had a one-to-one helper, as her statement specified, she could have been got out of the way. However, she was unattended and the chair ran into her, cutting a four-inch gash down the side of her face and narrowly missing her right eye.

Cara came home white and shocked, with a huge dressing on the side of her face and the prediction that she would probably be left with a scar. Although the mark of the injury faded over time, it was still sometimes noticeable even up to when she died.

David had a long telephone conversation with the new head, who had just been appointed, and demanded that the school adhere to the provision of a one-to-one helper. She said helplessly that she did not have the budget, and David told her that it was up to her to find it. We were not sure what the next stage would be, but we were soon to find out, because at the beginning of the summer holidays, another brown envelope landed on the doormat.

The senior official at the SEN department had decided to seize the moment. Far from expressing regret at what had happened, her response was to reiterate that she had never considered Sarah Millman the right school for Cara, and since it was now obvious that the LEA had been right all along, she proposed, with the head's consent, to withdraw Cara from the school and place her in Coquet Vale at the start of the autumn term.

(I should explain here that the LEA had in fact been in breach of Cara's statement by failing to provide a helper for her and that it is actually unlawful to remove a child from a school and simply transfer her to another without first changing the statement after a full review, including parental consultation.)

While I lay on my sofa fuming, David acted swiftly. He contacted one of our local representatives of IPSEA (Independent Panel for Special Education Advice), an organization that monitors the administration of SEN provision in local authorities. She immediately contacted the head of IPSEA at that time, and his response was rapid and effective. He sent us a copy of the fax he had sent to the legal department at the city council: since what they were proposing to do was in breach of the Education Act, the council should consider if it was the appropriate course of action, because if it proceeded any further, then IPSEA was prepared to take them to court on our behalf. Nowadays, David says he wishes that we had just let them do the transfer and had the court case, with all the ensuing publicity. However, we did not have the luxury of playing the legal games, because it was essential that things stay quiet until the baby was born, and as long as I was pregnant, we had to go for the easiest solutions.

In the end, after spinning things out as long as possible, the LEA did finally and very reluctantly back down. We did not, however, learn until the beginning of term that they had definitely abandoned their plans for a summary transfer to Coquet Vale.

I had started my pregnancy in a high state of anxiety, as worried as I had been about the previous one, if not more so. At the beginning, all I could do was play Solitaire obsessively, because even reading couldn't help me to relax. I knew I should calm down, but I couldn't, and as before, the anxiety became a vicious circle. Prayer was almost impossible for me, but oddly enough for a Protestant, I discovered the Divine Mercy prayer, which consisted merely of the words 'Jesus, I trust in you'. That was the whole of my prayer for most of my pregnancy, a general, brief but profound act of faith that gave voice to all my worries without allowing them to take over, and it was sufficient. What had happened before did not happen again. When I reached twenty-four weeks I began to breathe again, because now, whatever happened, the baby was viable.

I had monthly scans, kept my maternity appointments, and it seemed that all was well. I had refused any prenatal testing. Abortion was definitely not an option and if we were going to have another child with difficulties, we would deal with it if and when it happened. Until then, I would put my trust in God and live from day to day. It may seem strange to many people that I felt this way, but after having struggled so hard to get pregnant and stay pregnant, I could not have contemplated giving up the baby, whom I saw as a genuine miracle, something that had happened as the result of God's extraordinary grace.

There was a buzz of conspiratorial excitement in the air at the beginning of the spring term in our house, as Cara's social services helpers got her ready and David lifted her into our car instead of the usual taxi. This was because Cara was going to Northern Counties for an intensive three-day assessment, to help us prepare her altered statement. We had simply told her school that Cara was going for some further tests, because we had become very mistrustful of how far up the hierarchy the truth would go.

Cara enjoyed her three days at Northern Counties. The staff pinpointed, among other things, that she was touch-sensitive: although she liked to explore things with her hands, she would also withdraw from too much stimulation and so needed a tailored programme to enable her to use her hands more efficiently. It was recommended that Assisted Augmentative Communication should be used with her; this is a system of communication therapy that uses a mixture of methods tailored to each child's needs by an experienced teacher in close contact. Again, regular and detailed input from an occupational therapist was recommended, but we knew this was highly unlikely as long as she stayed in Sunderland.

Also prescribed was the daily programmed use of dark-ness and light therapy to specifically address her visual impairment problems, to a level that we knew would be difficult to provide in Sunderland, because we had had to go to Glasgow to get an accurate diagnosis of her difficulties from Professor Gordon Dutton, a world expert in cortical visual impairment. In the view of the school also, hydro-therapy several times a week and daily physio workouts were essential not only to develop the movement she still had, but also to keep her healthy; we knew that, based on our past experiences, these could not be guaranteed in Sunderland.

David asked for a meeting with the statement writer with the objective of incorporating the advice given to us by Northern Counties and also with the objective of making much more specific the identification of Cara's difficulties and the provision necessary to address them. At the end of a gruelling three-hour meeting, the writer finally admitted that her hands were tied by her managers. The following week, the statement was returned to us following a meeting with the senior SEN official, who had overturned everything David had asked for.

We were entitled to a second statement meeting, so David scheduled it for December. In the meantime, he spoke to several of Cara's therapists. One, in the Speech and Language Therapy department, told him when he asked for information to be made more specific, that she had been expressly warned not to specify and quantify therapy by the LEA hierarchy, because it bound them to deliver a legal requirement. Everything David asked to be included in the statement was eventually refused on the grounds of 'lack of evidence', this despite the supporting evidence from Professor Dutton at Glasgow and the very detailed information given by the teachers and therapists at Northern Counties.

I think that the LEA would say that we had unrealistic expectations for Cara and that no-one could have expected them to do everything that we wanted. As far as we are concerned, however, we did what all good parents do: we believed in our child. For us, faith in Cara was a given, as it is for all committed parents; we didn't even have to think about it, any more than we had to think twice about buying her pretty clothes or feeding and washing her. We did what lots of people do: we asked the questions, wrote the letters, asked to see the people in charge. If Cara had been a gifted child or even a well child, no-one would have thought that there was anything strange about what we were trying to do. But because she was at the other end of the scale altogether, we suddenly became 'difficult', 'awkward' or 'in denial'.

We blame no-one for the fact that Cara was so severely disabled and we blame no-one for the fact that they couldn't make her better. But what we do blame them for is that no-one tried, and that throughout Cara's life, no-one who had the power to help really thought that she was worth educating.

In the era of the European Convention on Human Rights, which specifies an education as a fundamental right of everyone in the European Community and which requires the state to respect the right of parents to have their children educated in line with their own philosophical and religious principles, the LEA's agenda seemed to be that our daughter would be entertained, cared for, given therapy (providing therapists were cheap and available) and thrown the odd bit of money for equipment or a trip out, but she was not to be 'educated' in the way that parents of well children would understand the term.

It has become possible to test for many genetic defects and to offer terminations to women who choose not to bring a child with severe difficulties into the world. Setting aside the ethical and emotional arguments surrounding abortion, however, there are still children born with conditions for which no tests are possible, children damaged at or after birth, and increasing numbers with severe autism. Surely, then, the most humane thing to do is for the state to put some serious resources into improving their capabilities. Had Cara been taught even to indicate when she was hungry or thirsty, or when she needed the toilet, how much easier all our lives would have been.

For Christians, there is a bigger picture here. Both the Old and the New Testaments set an intrinsic value on a human life regardless of its abilities or perceived attributes: human life is precious because God created it in his image in the beginning, and continues through successive generations of human history to sustain it. We are told by the psalmist that God is involved even in the formation of the child in the womb, that he sees the days ordained for a human life before they have even happened (Psalm 139). The incarnation of Jesus sends a message to all humanity that we are all valuable, and for Christians, disability has to be seen first and foremost in this context.

I do not believe that God 'caused' Cara to be born with a severe disability but that such afflictions are part of a flawed cosmos in the process of re-creation. My understanding of the life of Jesus is that he came to draw us, in however small a capacity, into this healing, restorative process, where even a tragedy as apparently hopeless as Cara's carries the possibility of redemption. Those directly involved with the disabled are given the opportunity to be involved in a uniquely challenging and rewarding creative endeavour, and many people, including our wonderful helpers, readily acknowledge this, even if they are not particularly religious. But the additional tragedy for families like ours is that many people in official positions give a good impression of being unaware of this vision and unwilling even to look at the possibility of a more humane approach.

I believe that it is the responsibility of all Christians involved with the disabled to seek to become part of this dynamic, to assist God's plans for them as individuals and to test all policies, proposals, laws and procedures in our secular society against God's standards. Because we live in a world that is usually against the values of God's kingdom, that is inevitably going to be hard and sometimes may seem impossible, but the stand still has to be made.

Christmas came and went, and the weeks went on, and I got bigger and bigger. I was already scheduled for a Caesarean delivery, and our second daughter arrived on 9 March 2005. Because we considered her to be such a miracle, we had already decided to call her Charis, meaning 'grace', and added Julia and Rose, one after our gynaecologist, and the other a family name. She looked a thousand years old when she entered the world, cried for about two minutes and then stopped as she became too busy watching everything around her. She was totally unlike Cara (only 7 lb 7 oz), bald, wrinkled, skinny, and with penetrating blue eyes and an uncanny resemblance in her first hours of life to David's late father in one of his fiercer moods. Three years on, she still thinks she knows far more than the rest of us, though fortunately, she is now a chubby, fair-skinned and very pretty red-blonde, with a cupid-bow mouth. She is healthy, bright and very good company. She is a sign to us that life goes on and that God's compassion never ends.

The only things that happened in the early part of the year were that an independent physiotherapist came to assess Cara to write a report for her statement, and David took a further trip to Glasgow to have Cara reassessed by Professor Dutton. We tried to get an independent speech and language therapist but were told by one of them that no-one who worked within the area would challenge a local LEA in case it affected his or her chances of employment. An independent educational psychologist proved too expensive. We began to realize dimly just how difficult it was going to be to prepare a convincing case to send Cara to Northern Counties when we had such limited financial resources.

It was nevertheless a hopeful time because of Charis, who continued to delight us day by day. I had a deep sense that something very important had been accomplished; we had at last completed our family against all the odds and now I could get on with my own life. I did not want to go straight back into my old career and began to pray seriously about what I should do next. One day when I was out walking the dog, the idea popped into my head that I should think about a career of some kind that involved law. I wanted to be able to access legal advice easily, because the difficulties we had had were not just going to go away.

We met up with Cara's godmother one day. I mentioned that I wanted to do some kind of law course and she looked surprised. 'Oh, I'm doing a paralegal course soon,' she said. 'It's for people involved with community groups and voluntary services – I could send you the details over the Net if you like.'

So it was that I ended up doing a course that I later described as an Alpha course for people who know nothing about the legal system. It had been organized by Sunderland Council for Voluntary Services with a development trust and had been put together by a solicitor who felt that community groups needed to be better informed about their rights and responsibilities and thus be better equipped to take on local authorities and other agencies. As we were preparing for Cara's tribunal during the first term, I found the course both a necessary distraction and of some help in our enterprise, though maybe it would have been better if the tribunal had come later in the year.

There were some major upheavals at church too. It had been decided the previous year that the best way to deal with the large numbers of people coming to our church on a Sunday morning was to set up a new church in Sunderland. Our current pastor would lead it and he would be replaced at the home church by a new pastor, who would be coming in September. We had heard the new pastor preach in April and wanted him to do Charis's dedication.

Sadly, this was not possible. Of course, these events inevitably created a lot of instability, especially for those left in the old church. In our extremely difficult personal circumstances, we were under particular pressure in any case, and though we stayed, we found it very hard. After almost a year, when an unexpected problem arose over Charis's dedication, and close to Cara's tribunal hearing, we finally decided that it was time to leave.

I once heard a sermon by Tommy Tenney, in my God Channel days, in which he compared local churches to bakeries. The importance of bread is unconsciously accepted by everyone, and everyone knows where to get it. Many of us have memories of real home-baked bread or of bread snacks of one kind or another, such as the sugar on bread and butter I was given as a very small child, or the soggy breadsticks clutched by weaning babies; the advertising market taps into this nostalgia so effectively.

A church should offer the Bread of Life. In other words, if a church is really living out the life of Christ, then that process will be palpable and will attract people naturally; they will follow where they see Jesus.

In a situation like the one we were all in, it is hard for any church to provide for the needs of everyone in the congregation, and for us, it seemed right to move to a more stable place. Oddly enough, the solution seemed to simply drop into our hands. We had from time to time sneaked off to St Nicholas's in the marketplace at Durham, a Victorian gem of a church which, being Evangelical Anglican, was rather like Dr Who's Tardis inside, because it found room for so many activities and functions.

We found the atmosphere restful to the spirit and a spur to all kinds of interesting possibilities – warm-hearted and grown-up. By mutual agreement, we approached the vicar, who, after a lengthy discussion of our difficulties, said that he could offer us a blessing and thanksgiving service at 'St Nic's'.

So it was that in September 2005, Charis was blessed and given thanks for under the auspices of the Church of England at Durham. Because of our preoccupation with Cara, however, it took us a while to build relationships at

St Nic's, and despite some extremely good worship and teaching during this period, we felt rather out on our own as we prepared Cara's case, I did my course assignments and we waited for the tribunal.

# 7  Tribunal and Aftermath

One summer Sunday, as other people's lawnmowers purred and other people's children listened for the ice cream van, we sat down with Cara's files and began to collate the correspondence in date order, year by year, from our first encounters with the local authority. It took us five hours altogether to sort everything out so that it could be sent off to SENDIST, the Special Educational Needs and Disability Tribunal, for them to collate into a case bundle. Cara rolled cheerfully on her play mat as we spread the numerous letters, reports and assessments all over the floor, because there were too many to put on the dining table.[1]

The tribunal panel is composed of three people: an overseeing lawyer, who acts as chair, and two professionals with experience of special needs education. Additionally, the two professionals must have a minimum of six years' experience working, not in the charitable sector, but in local authority education. It is supposed to be informal; it allows the use of hearsay evidence which does not have to be corroborated by witnesses; it is usually held in a hotel conference room; it keeps personnel down to a minimum and makes no use of the usual legal paraphernalia such as gowns, wigs or court layout. It is supposed to allow free discussion and a certain amount of dialogue between the opposing parties, because the ideal is that they will be able to come to agreement. However, whatever else it may be, relaxed and unbuttoned it is not, because too much depends on the outcome. Parent representatives are not included on the tribunal panel, which makes me wonder how impartial it can really be. The lack of formality also allows a degree of imprecision and flexibility in discussion that does not always work to a child's advantage and that would probably not be allowed to pass unchallenged in normal court proceedings.

The deputy head of Northern Counties School had told us that she was retiring and that the new head, Judith, would be accompanying us as our witness on the day. She was confident that Judith would be able to handle the task, and was equally confident that we had a good chance of winning; if a child with Cara's level of difficulty could not be given a chance to go to Northern Counties, then who could?

So, on a chilly morning in October, I put on my black trouser suit, and David his best suit and tie, and we headed off to the hotel beside the central station in Newcastle. We were extremely apprehensive.

We met Judith for the first time and very quickly established a good relationship with her; she was young, frank and very down-to-earth. Small, slim, with a turned-up nose and thick bobbed hair, she exuded energy and confidence and was a powerfully good influence on us as the day went on.

The SEN Head appeared and greeted us coolly, as did the Coquet Vale head teacher, Mr Weaver, who subsequently buried himself in *The Times Educational Supplement*. Their third witness was the senior educational psychologist.

We were ushered into the conference room set aside for us, and the tribunal began. We were ranged on one side of the table, and the panel on the other, and there were times when, from our point of view, it felt like the Spanish Inquisition.

The team consisted of Mr Chisholm, a retired headmaster who looked rather like the moustached town clerk in the TV comedy *Dad's Army* and emerged as having a mindset from the same period; Ms Scorton, stout, florid and very keen on writing things down; and the chair, Mr Blenkinsopp. He was a little man with large ears and tiny hands and feet, who was immune to anything but the most finely tuned and technical legal argument – as far as we were concerned, that is. Additionally, there was a clerk, and an observer in training.

The LEA representatives started with the assertion that Northern Counties did not have the correct designation to take a child like Cara. The session was immediately adjourned so that Judith could check that the designation had definitely been changed with the DfES; this information came through after about twenty minutes from the school. The LEA team were then immediately on the back foot, because they had expected to go home and instead had to face a blow-by-blow dissection from our side, in which Cara's difficulties were redefined to what we felt was an acceptable level. Part 2 of the statement (which defines the child's difficulties) was therefore largely taken care of in the first half of the morning and in a way that made us feel cautiously optimistic. We had got most of what we wanted, and the LEA people were looking very dismal when we saw them in the hotel's dingy and uncomfortable coffee bar.

We went in to the Part 3 discussion with an increased sense of confidence and were cheered by our victory when Mr Blenkinsopp acidly pointed out to the SEN Head the section of the Code of Practice that insists that the LEA must specify and quantify therapies, and upheld our assertion that this needed to be done for Cara. Again, we were successful, and I began to hope that we would succeed overall, because the picture that was emerging did not put Sunderland LEA in a very good light at all. What I did not realize was that the chair was simply flexing his muscles and this did not mean automatically that Part 4, which dealt with the school choice, was going to be a foregone conclusion.

Where things started to unravel for us was at the continuation of the Part 3 discussion, after lunch, because it was here that the LEA unveiled their secret weapon. In essence, it was the ability of the head of Coquet Vale to flannel for more than two hours, so that the afternoon came to an end before we were allowed even to ask questions of him. If we had finished on that day, it is just possible we might have won.

The panel, with the utmost respect, asked Mr Weaver to talk about his school, without asking for any specific information.

'Well, er, obviously we have won lots of awards,' he began and proceeded to reel them off. Most were awarded by business organizations and had little obvious relevance to special education.

'Everything but the *Blue Peter* badge,' I murmured to Judith, but the panel were smiling and nodding.

'And then, of course,' he continued, 'we have, er, considerable experience of an, er, emotional intelligence programme developed at the school.'

'Perhaps you'd like to tell us about it, Mr Weaver,' said Ms Scorton brightly, as he appeared to run out of words.

'Well, um, we tend to try to suit it to every child. Every child, we believe, can succeed in this area, even if they do have learning difficulties. It's, er, suited to every child working at their own pace. Of the utmost importance. We place a high priority on this.' The phrases came haltingly, like water out of an air-locked tap. At the end, we were certainly no wiser as to what was meant by 'emotional intelligence' and I doubt if the panel were.

'Then, of course, you see, um, lots of children have come to the school unable to do anything, but we find they do well once they are there.'

'Could you give us some examples of that, Mr Weaver?' I asked.

'I'm sorry, Mrs Tolchard, I can't allow you to interrupt at this point,' said Mr Blenkinsopp, smoothly. 'You will have your chance later.'

No examples were forthcoming. 'Of course, Cara would be in a class with very similar children. Now, let me see, there's, er, yes, I do have a class list with me.' He scrutinized it. 'Oh, um, no, I'm afraid this is last year's. Never mind. Now, is Uzma still in the class? Yes, she is. And Ryan and, er, Louise. I think. No. No – she moved on.' He continued in this vein until he had gone through the list, omitting to give us any diagnostic information about the children.

The observer, who was sitting at the end of the table, well out of the way, by this time had an incredulous smirk on her face.

He moved on to visual impairment facilities. 'Well, um, we do have a light room. And we have a very experienced teaching assistant whose specialism is, er, light.' He chose not to give us any further information on this but opened and closed his mouth a few times, having clearly run out of things to say.

'I think Mr and Mrs Tolchard have concerns about Cara being appropriately stimulated in class, Mr Weaver,' said Ms Scorton. 'How would you respond to that?'

'Oh, well, as a matter of fact, I'm a great believer in children having a rest.' He sat up suddenly, displaying the first sign of conviction and energy that had appeared so far. 'There are children who often fall asleep in school and, if I may say so, *are the better for it!*' He looked proudly at the panel, as if expecting another award.

I glanced at the observer, who at this point had her head down and, with shaking shoulders, was struggling to contain her laughter.

We weren't laughing. 'I can't listen to this,' I whispered to David. We stood up.

'I'm sorry,' said David firmly. 'I don't think we can cope with this.'

For the first time, Mr Blenkinsopp appeared slightly worried. 'You must stay,' he said. 'It would be better for your case if you do. Please.'

After a long moment we obediently resumed our seats.

After the howler about sleeping in class, Mr Weaver proceeded to drone on until the end of the afternoon in the same vein. Whenever we tried to ask questions, we were smartly slapped down by Mr Blenkinsopp. We had to listen to Mr Weaver failing to tell the panel any of the qualifications of his teachers – 'very experienced' was all he would say – and when questioned about health and safety in view of Cara's accident, he pursed his lips and said sagely, 'Vigilance. Vigilance.' (We were to discover later that at the time the school had no written health and safety policy.) By this time, the observer had recovered her self-control and was scribbling away dutifully, though at times with both eyebrows raised. The light was failing and I stared out of the window, willing him to stop talking.

He said with great pride that the school was very keen on taking the children out on visits, even though we had already established that Cara's health was too vulnerable in cold weather for her to be outside for prolonged periods of time and this was to be written in to Part 2, which described her difficulties. What few facts did emerge from his speech horrified us; they were the antithesis of everything that we wanted for Cara, and showed us how right we had been to insist that she did not attend before. It was farcical, it was egregiously unfair, it was heartbreaking – but it was permitted, because as we look back now, I think we realize that, unless we had been able to provide evidence that Cara would miraculously improve if she attended Northern Counties, the panel were always going to support the LEA.

At last Mr Blenkinsopp called a halt and said that we would reconvene in December. We had no alternative but to comply. We were still hopeful, but it was becoming harder to be so when we saw that our objections to the school, which were perfectly reasonable and valid to us and probably to many people, apparently carried no weight in the parallel universe of state-run education for SEN pupils.

At the meeting in December – same time, same awful place – we were finally allowed to ask our questions, but there was a sense that no-one was really listening. Everyone on our team commented both on the day and afterwards that the climate seemed to have changed. From being listened to attentively on the first day and having most of what we asked for granted, we had moved to a situation where the attitude of the panel towards us was dismissive; it is hard not to feel that the decision had already been predetermined.

I provided a clear summary of our objections, which the panel agreed to accept, but I think we had lost by then anyway. The SEN Head stood up and promised rather lamely that, yes, he would provide an occupational therapist, even if he had to pay privately (even though Cara had needed one for the past four years), and yes, he would ensure that a professionally qualified speech therapist was available for the hours specified in Part 3. And the panel, ex-LEA employees as they were, nodded and smiled and accepted what he said.

I realize that there are some parents who have achieved what they wanted and who feel that justice was granted to them and their children by SENDIST. But we believe that the process of forming a judgment in Cara's case was deeply flawed, even perverse, and that the final conclusion was arrived at by deliberately overlooking not only Mr Weaver's apparent lack of knowledge about provision, but the evidence we provided of the absence of good faith on the part of the LEA.

We were left to wait a fortnight before we got the bad news. We were nervous wrecks when the judgment came in, two days before Christmas. We had achieved almost everything we wanted in parts 2 and 3, but the thing that would have made it happen, sending Cara to Northern Counties, was denied us: 'We can find no reason to assume that Cara would significantly improve if sent to Northern Counties.' In other words, the choice of Cara's school was not dependent on her level of need or on her entitlement to an education, but on whether or not there would be tangible benefits in sending her outside the state system; she only deserved a decent education if she was 'worthy' of it. Because the appeal process was then unclear and had little chance of success, when we subsequently appealed, we failed.

At the time, I was too shattered to think about doing anything apart from crawling into a hole. We had never felt so utterly discouraged since Cara's diagnosis; in fact, this was worse, because people had had the chance to help her and had deliberately chosen to pass it up. The sense of betrayal and of what we felt was the abdication of responsibility towards Cara and us by the system, was deep and poisonous, because it cut across every assumption that most people naively hold about the law, that it assigns justice to the innocent and protects them from those who do wrong.

The world was a very bleak place for us then and it was undoubtedly our worst Christmas since becoming parents, even though we of course had Charis and we tried to celebrate for her sake. I sat in the Christmas morning service at St Nic's with the tears quietly rolling down my face. I knew that to ask why God had allowed it to happen was a redundant question, though I did ask him why, when we had been so close, he had allowed us to lose. I knew in theory that God would bring good out of it somehow, but I couldn't see how. All I could see was the loss of every chance Cara would have had in a school like Northern Counties and the horror of her being sent back to the same people who had failed us before.

After the night we got the decision, when I had sat up late alternating glasses of sherry and Baileys, weeping and watching television without taking in a word of it, I realized that I needed to take myself in hand. I knew that if I didn't get help, I was probably heading for some kind of breakdown. I went to the doctor's and asked to be put on antidepressants, not the maximum dose but a fairly large one, enough to take the edge off the pain to allow me to function from day to day. Unlike my doctor at the beginning, she understood exactly where I was coming from. If enough people ignore you and disregard your opinion, you begin to feel that you are worthless: the drug stopped me from perpetually spending my time blaming myself because we hadn't won this battle either. I was inwardly as frantic as only a parent can be when her deepest instincts about her child are set aside, so it was important that some of the emotion be taken away.

David, who had once been so insouciant and optimistic, wasn't as emotionally fragile as I was, but he was profoundly bitter and angry. For a while he refused to discuss it, but then, like me, he began to look at what we could realistically do now. Even in the state we were in, we were not going to simply sit back and do nothing. This new goal gave us something to focus on and a reason to go on, and in the end, I think it saved our sanity.

# 8  Kung Fu Fighting

The days between Christmas and New Year found our family snugly insulated in the car, driving through swirling snow-storms to Northumberland. In theory, we wanted to begin our search for a new place to live; at an emotional level, we needed to get out of Sunderland for a while and regroup. It was bleak but restorative, a winter mini-adventure, as in C. S. Lewis's *The Silver Chair*, or *Sir Gawain and the Green Knight*, a quest to keep us focused when other families were still eating turkey sandwiches and mince pies in front of the television.

In the first week of the New Year we sought publicity in the local newspapers for what had happened, which we had never done before. We had a beautiful little girl and we decided that maybe it was time to publicize just how raw a deal she was getting from the people who were supposed to be helping her. I didn't achieve everything I wanted, but I did manage to have articles on Cara run in the *Sunderland Echo* and, with the help of a journalist friend of ours, in the *Newcastle Chronicle* and *Journal*. The articles focused on the benefits she would have got from going to Northern Counties and the extreme misgivings we had about sending her to Coquet Vale, with particular reference to her communication problem. They were accompanied by some beautiful pictures of her, and were presented with taste and respect.

We said in the articles that we were planning to move because we despaired of finding an appropriate education for Cara in Sunderland, and we meant it. I mourned our lovely house, but with David I did the homework on opportunities available in other areas.

One almost immediate good result of this strategy was that Northern Counties, impressed by our initiative and the good things we said about them, helped us to get some much-needed legal advice free of charge, and Judith herself wrote a letter for inclusion in our case saying that the decision of the tribunal to send Cara to Coquet Vale did not accurately reflect the discussion that had taken place. Because I was doing my paralegal course, I was advised to collect as much evidence as I could of any failings on the part of the LEA to provide what parts 2 and 3 of the statement required, to demand access to therapy programmes, timetables, Cara's daily routines and details of professional visits, and in short to demonstrate that, whatever the school thought, we did not believe that the statement was just a formality.

David was back into work and was using it to forget as much as he could what was going on, and although I was so bitter against the legal system that I had thought about dropping out of the course, I continued with it on the basis that it just might help us in the long run. It was vitally important for me at this time to be able to concentrate on something apart from Cara, and as the course went on and more of it got absorbed into my psyche, I also began to find it a very useful and powerful mental discipline. If I could look at a case and start to analyse it in cold legal terms, then it gave me a measure of control over it; also, it meant that I had to engage my reason, and anything that made me do that helped greatly with the depression and anxiety that I lived with.

Retrospectively, I know that our outcome at tribunal would have been much better if we had hired a good education lawyer, who could have argued much more knowledgeably and on equal terms with the panel on our behalf; statistically (and paradoxically, given the current trend to de-professionalize legal processes), many more tribunals are won by parents who use professional legal services, and the financial cost would have been well worth it. We almost won as it was; professional help would probably have given us the result we wanted.

The amended statement naming Coquet Vale arrived through our letter box in the second week in January. I say 'amended', but in fact it was still the copy of the original one with the amendments written in over the previous words. No-one had had time to type a new copy because Cara had to start at her new school as quickly as possible to comply with the tribunal ruling.

I was forced to be reconciled for the moment, because I couldn't afford to give way to how I was feeling. The initial hurt and grief transmuted into cold logic, by no means an ideal way to conduct a relationship, but a useful way of surviving. I wonder, in retrospect, how the tribunal panel could have believed that there was even a hope of this placement working out satisfactorily when there was so much disagreement on both sides.

The difficulties started almost immediately. In Cara's first week, we were sent a consent form asking us to give permission for Cara to go on out-of-school visits every Tuesday. I returned it the next day with a refusal, explaining our concerns about Cara's tendency to chest infections. The next day brought a letter from the head asking if we would please change our minds, as the visits were a vital part of the curriculum. I wrote back again, this time in a personal letter to the head, referring him to the discussion at the tribunal about Cara's health and to the part of the statement that said that we did not want her to go out of school in cold weather because of her propensity to infections and accompanying seizures. I thought that the matter was closed – until I then received a note from Cara's class teacher asking the same thing. I took a deep breath and wrote another letter explaining why she couldn't go, referring her to the statement. Throughout the term, they continued to try to push us, even though it was one of the coldest springs on record.

I did not sign the Home-School Agreement promising to ensure Cara's good behaviour in school, on the basis that Cara was not capable of behavioural problems and that it was therefore not relevant. I wanted to do nothing that could be construed from a legal point of view as giving consent to the placement.

This cautious and formal procedure on our part was predetermined by the legal advice we had been given, which was to make sure that every exchange between us and the school and LEA was clearly recorded and copied, with no room for any ambiguity or deniability. The circumstances we were in sadly did not allow a friendly, relaxed relationship.

The school brochure claimed that every child who went there got a 'bespoke' educational programme specifically designed to meet his or her needs. But we did not find this to be true; what seemed to happen in practice, during Cara's time there, was that things that worked with some children were then offered to every child on an ad hoc, experimental basis.

One of the few things Cara seemed to enjoy and to respond to was the use of sound-beam therapy, a game using light and sound, which made use of her excellent hearing and helped her with an awareness of cause and effect. She was given it for half an hour a week, but when we asked if this could be extended, we were refused. The reason given was that she 'might get bored' with it, but when David asked the therapist about it, she admitted that it was because the therapy was given to every child and more time for Cara could not be fitted in. Then there was the attempt to introduce aromatherapy to Cara at lunchtimes 'to relax her', which we vetoed, first, because the ongoing problem with Cara was keeping her stimulated, and secondly, because many aromatherapists will not treat epileptics in case the oils bring on seizures.

There were many instances of this kind of thing. Every time, we had to try to discover why things were being proposed, and when members of staff were challenged, they frequently could not give good reasons.

Even in terms of keeping us informed, the school fell short. When we wanted to check how often reviews of Cara's programmes were done, because the statement stipulated set times for some of them, we were told that the school did not keep records of professional visits. Her end-of-term and half-termly reviews were missed, and the minutes did not appear until the beginning of the following term, even though we were supposed to have an input. It felt increasingly as though a deliberate policy of conceal-ment might be going on. At the beginning of Cara's second year, our requests for a new timetable met with another long delay and the surprised admission from her new class teacher that no-one else had ever asked for one before. The school very clearly expected little or no involvement from parents in the implementation of their children's statements.

It was exactly as we had feared: the worst possible place for a child like Cara, a child with 'special special needs', a child who needed a very high level of routine, repetition, and close and careful monitoring by people who knew exactly what they were doing, if she was ever to make any progress.

From being a happy, outgoing child who squealed with pleasure when the taxi came to take her to school, and was full of activity and smiles when she came home, Cara turned very quickly into a quiet, resigned, serious little girl who was not the child we had known. Because initially the school did not even stick to her timetable, I think that probably at the beginning, she was disorientated, and later perhaps even depressed by the noisy, constantly changing environment. We know that she was well liked and that many of the staff tried hard with her, but it wasn't enough. I dealt daily with the personal pain, because I knew that she wasn't happy and it wasn't within my power to change things for her.

Remembering it all now, I can see just how bad it was, but at the time, hope and a positive attitude had become a way of life for us, and practical perseverance a daily recourse. I had to stay on my pills, and David was now being treated for high blood pressure, but we managed and we still had a life. Having Charis helped, because there was a strong sense of life going on as usual even in the bizarre set of circumstances with Cara that we had to endure. Charis was now approaching one year, wide-eyed, chunky, adorable, and we cherished every moment with her because we had experienced nothing like it with Cara.

As I had thrown myself into finding a therapy programme for Cara, I now threw myself into building a case to get her out of Coquet Vale. I found a solicitor who gave us advice on how much more information we needed to support our arguments. I remember questioning Cara's class teacher and the deputy head very closely at a review meeting at the beginning of the summer term, David in attendance. Everything we heard only confirmed us in our opinion that they were struggling in their understanding of Cara's problems and had limited facilities and no specialisms that could be of much use to her. I spent hours recording the shortfalls in therapy provision. When our solicitor wrote an official letter of complaint to the LEA detailing their shortcomings, I think they finally realized how serious we were.

The school year ended not with a bang but a whimper: our solicitor finally said that, although there was substantial evidence of failure to meet statement provisions, we did not have a clear enough case to get us legal aid for a judicial review of the tribunal decision; incredibly, the longer the failures were allowed to continue, the better our case would be. Even the previous year, I would have bitten pieces out of the carpet in sheer frustration, but instead I just carried on. By this time, even David's optimism was buckling, but oddly enough, I, the confirmed pessimist and hand-wringer, absolutely refused to accept that we couldn't do anything. At the very least, Cara's statutory assessment at the end of primary school would happen in two years and we could have another crack at Northern Counties then.

Looking back now, I am glad that I no longer have to live this way. It really was a war of attrition, with absolute commitment on both sides to our own agendas. But how much energy could have been better spent resolving Cara's difficulties than arguing about them! How much more time I could have spent with Cara rather than hunched over my computer upstairs writing letters; I regret now that I wasn't with her more and that when I was with her, I spent my time turning over how best to help her. But at the time, there seemed to be no other way. I think that if I had been less detached and more involved with Cara on a personal level, I couldn't have survived; the pain would have disabled me, and the situation simply did not allow me to be just a mum.

I regret also that the school and the authority only ever saw the side of us, and of me in particular, that was tough and unyielding. I would have greatly preferred it if, at the forefront of our actions, we could have kept some sense of the fact that we were all human beings. But the situation and the extreme vulnerability of our position did not seem to allow it; signs of conciliation in the early days had been exploited to Cara's disadvantage. Soldiers in combat are there to fight, and that was the situation we felt we were in. It is impossible to fight nicely.

At church, we had now become part of a house group, and I belonged to a small women's prayer group that met fortnightly on Thursday mornings. Nothing dramatic happened, but for me there was a powerful sense of spiritual reconnection and a tremendous feeling of unobtrusive emotional support that fed me at a deep level and helped me to survive some of the worst disappointments. Like us, no-one knew what the future held, but we were accepted and loved anyway, even when we weren't feeling especially spiritual or capable of putting a Christian framework on what was happening to us. I particularly loved my small group, which consisted of three other mothers, and there was a genuine sense of God working through it.

Now there was almost nothing else in my focus, apart from getting my paralegal qualification, as the course was drawing to an end. The downside of finishing, of course, was that I could no longer escape into my Wednesday mornings, with all the banter and chit-chat, but the upside was that I became more confident in my general understanding of Cara's case. Although I knew that there was a huge amount that I didn't know, I began to believe that maybe we did have a fighting chance after all.

Somehow, we had been expecting a more spruced-up version of Cara's statement at some point, and when it didn't appear, I wrote a letter to the SEN Head asking for it. It was exactly the same as the previous one, with handwritten amendments that had never been properly typed out. I was flicking through it when I noticed some private documents at the end of the bundle that had been copied and sent to us by mistake. Among these was an email pre-dating the tribunal that offered some interesting insights into their strategy.

One sentence in particular jumped out, in response to our requests for additional needs to be included in Part 2: 'If it is not going to make any material difference to the placement etc. (no hostages to fortune, would not require additional provision in Part 3, just an issue of semantics) then I think we should write it in – that has been the strategy so far.'

So there it was: the SEN department did not want David's suggested alterations included in the statement if this meant more provision was required, which naturally would require more resources, though they were willing to write them in if it was 'just an issue of semantics' that would not require any 'hostages to fortune'. Our solicitor, to whom we showed it, read it in context as an interference with the statutory process of statement writing.

It made me curious to find out what other materials might be lurking in Cara's files. So I filled out an application for access to the records held for Cara by the LEA under the Data Protection Act. It took months of dispute before I was given them, but they contained some very interesting items, such as a letter from the SEN Head to the educational psychologist that showed that the decision to send Cara to Coquet Vale was as much a surprise to him as it was to us. I added the documents to my files and wrote a letter of complaint about the email.

There was one interesting diversion in the earlier part of the year that made us at least temporarily look beyond our own immediate problems. Judith James called us one day from Northern Counties and said that David Cameron, who had then just been elected leader of the Conservative Party, was coming to view the school on a visit that had been arranged prior to some local elections. The school was trying to arrange a brief forum for parents to be able to talk to him about the difficulties they were experiencing with the state system, and would we like to attend? Of course we said yes; no-one knew very much about him then, but he had achieved a modest amount of fame among the parents of disabled children, because, as the father of a severely disabled child himself (now sadly deceased), as a local MP he had made it his business to oppose the closure of special schools, so, rightly or otherwise, we regarded him as something of an ally.

Much has been written about 'the Cameron effect' in the early days of David Cameron's leadership. We were all in a small room, sitting on the floor with our children when he came in and sat down with us, indicating as he did so that the television cameras should leave, and all of us had a chance to express our particular difficulties. He told us, a little self-consciously, that he wanted to centralize SEN assessment so that there was no longer the capability for the local authority to save money by failing to identify children's difficulties and that he hoped to prevent any further school closures and to support schools like Northern Counties and Percy Hedley.

As the discussion broadened, I thought he looked quite overwhelmed by the burden of expectation from all of us desperate parents, and very serious; he did not make use of any easy clichés, and his large, expressive eyes registered a real compassion for our children's difficulties.

It was extremely interesting to see someone at that early stage in their political career. I think all of us warmed to him and felt that, at that point at least, he was a genuine person who was trying hard to understand the issues and who felt, if anything, slightly awkward about his public-school background and aristocratic connections. It is always a mistake to believe that any single political party or figure has all the answers, but I hope he remembers us and continues to try to improve things for our children.

Earlier in this chapter, I mentioned that we were fighting this year on two fronts. I have described the first one at some length, but so far I haven't referred to our other area of difficulty: Cara's care and occupational therapy provision. This, the next conflict, was just about to blow up and take up almost as much time as the fight over Cara's education.

Part 3

The Second Front

# 9  A Matter of Caring

When a child is tiny, it is second nature for any reasonable parent to provide total care, taking care of feeding, washing, changing and all the other practical and potentially messy jobs that go with parenthood. Mum or Dad may argue about who does it, but it gets done because we are, by and large, wired up to take care of little ones. Because of their size, they are relatively easy to lift, feed and clean up, and even those parents who find the whole process of toddler-taming repugnant can comfort themselves with the knowledge that eventually Junior will probably get the hang of doing those things for himself.

Cara was a model baby: pretty, quiet, never able to get grubby, never crying unless she was very poorly. She never showed signs of behavioural problems and was content with whatever you chose to do with her; I have a memory of her lying on the floor at six months, peacefully watching the prisms that I had hung in the window to stimulate her vision, utterly content. To her paediatrician's surprise, she did not need to use a feeding tube, and she ate everything with apparent enjoyment. She was never able to be toilet-trained, but nappies can be very useful when children are small.

This was very easy to deal with when Cara was a toddler, because all these things are the common lot of parents everywhere. But then she grew larger and it became harder to lift her; transportation facilities like pushchairs and car seats began to require a level of physical skill that Cara simply did not have, such as the ability to hold up her head or sit upright for long periods. Public changing facilities became too small; bought baby or toddler food was no longer suitable, so more forward planning was required every time we took her out.

We used nappies up to a maximum weight for much longer than they were effective, but it was many months before the Incontinence Service contacted us. Even going up and down stairs or giving Cara a bath suddenly became major feats of exertion as she grew lengthwise, taller than average for her age; her toddler bed was outgrown, but kept because it still needed to accommodate a child who was incapable of preventing herself from falling out and who, even with pads, could still make sheets and mattresses wet or smelly. She now required a car large enough to take a bigger and more specialized car seat; a hoist was now needed indoors because lifting her was becoming too difficult.

Medicines were now prescribed, not just those to deal with Cara's immediate conditions, such as epilepsy, but also those to offset the problems caused by her other medication and general immobility: laxatives, preventative antibiotics, ointments, antacids. Then latterly came puberty, with all the attendant issues of personal dignity and privacy that were no less important for Cara than for any other adolescent. These were the practical issues faced daily by us as Cara's parents, and in this area, as in others, there were varying standards of competence shown by the people who were supposed to provide the support.

I was never very good at the care side, because I have always been squeamish and I have certain physical issues myself that make heavy lifting undesirable. I used to get obsessively meticulous over the administration of medicines, and although I did all the other things, the sheet changing, the long hours of washing and drying and food preparation and cleaning up, and sometimes the changing of clothes and pads soaked with poo and vomit, I found it hard, even though I accepted it as part of life with Cara.

Surfing the Internet one day, I came across a website about St Thérèse of Lisieux. I immediately felt a connection with her, the saint of the unsung and the boring and the small things. Full of love and insight beyond her years, she believed that God cares less about what we do for him than about the love with which we do it. Grasping the concept of doing hidden, small things with love, the celebrated and spiritually ingenious 'Little Way', was an important development for someone like me, who had always been encouraged, both at home and at church, to aim for very visible success and achievement.

I tried to keep in mind the wider context of how God looked at my life: 'All our Lord does is right,' Thérèse also wrote, 'and everything he permits is worthwhile.'[1] Accepting from God's hand a life that seemed on the surface to be utterly fruitless and insignificant is one of the hardest things I have ever had to do, and it radically overturned my view of God to realize that, as far as he was concerned, it was also probably one of the most precious, to him and to my own growth in faith.

I coped well with Cara throughout her babyhood and during the time when she was a toddler, but I first remember finding the day-to-day care difficult when she was about four or five. Until then, we had always looked after Cara entirely by ourselves, and except for her hospital stays, she had never spent a night with anyone other than us. Apart from the periodic illnesses and accompanying seizures, the regime we had adopted worked well in keeping Cara healthy, so setting aside the worries that we learned to live with (up to a point), the most difficult things about life with Cara at this age were physical tiredness and the boredom of the daily routine.

When it became clear that the Doman-Delacato pro-grammes were only having a limited effect, my confidence and commitment flagged, and however much I loved Cara, I began to find daily life with her extremely monotonous. This feeling will be familiar to many mothers who, having fallen in love with their babies and devoted unstinting time and care to meeting their needs, suddenly wake up one morning and panic as they wonder where their own lives have gone.

The obvious thing to do for the mother of a well child is to find some good childcare and take a job that provides an outlet and a fulfilment for those needs that the child can't meet. For the mother of a disabled child, however, the solution is not so simple or so clear-cut. It is often hard to find a childminder who will take on an older disabled child, for one thing, especially one who is epileptic, incontinent and wheelchair-bound, and the proliferation of meetings and consultations, as well as time off when the child is ill, means that the mother requires a very tolerant employer, and perhaps a job that is not too stressful because so much of her time and energy can be consumed at home.

Cara's needs had become my full-time occupation and we were trying desperately to have another child. The sheer logistics of trying to set up some kind of care package with social services was just a step too far for us, as well as trying to organize alternatives if at times it couldn't be met. So we finally contacted social services with a view to getting some time off.

Our assigned social worker, Rebecca, was the best we ever had: young, full of common sense and intelligence, and with a view of the system that saw it as existing primarily to meet the needs of its clients; in the later climate of service cuts, we were to discover how rare this attitude is. She was smart, focused and practical, and approached our case with sensitivity and respect. Even Rebecca, however, was unable to find us very much initially.

When I finally became pregnant with Charis, however, it was clear that something needed to be done, because David, who by this time was not working from home, could no longer be there to get Cara up in the mornings or feed and change her at lunchtimes and teatimes. Eventually Rebecca managed to get her boss to agree to a contracted-out care service.

The private service that social services employed were extremely efficient not only at providing experienced workers, but also at matching the workers to the job. One of our first helpers was Janice, who had been a nanny to an aristocratic family and who kept us entertained with stories of her life among the upper classes; another was Linda, who was with Cara literally until her last hospital dash and who had also worked as a volunteer with children with disabilities.

They were very good at what they did. They were cheerful, sympathetic and extremely kind, and Cara herself enjoyed the playtimes that were incorporated into the care plan. Charis too, after she was born, benefited from having so many different people in the house to chat to her, and is still a confident and articulate child. The service they gave to Cara and me was invaluable.

Cara's paediatrician had gone on maternity leave. During this time, she was replaced by Dr Lee, who herself had a child with severe cerebral palsy and had had some experience of dealing with the inertia of the occupational therapy (OT) service where money was concerned. She told us that the abolition of the means test for house adaptations was very close and that we should try to get in quickly since there was likely to be a flood of applications. So David contacted the OT service again.

My hormones were distinctly awry and I was very conscious of being spotty, barefoot and pregnant, with untrimmed hair and no make-up when the new occupational therapist appeared at the house. I was to become unreasonably irritated by the fact that she seemed to appear in a new item of designer clothing every time we saw her; as well as my other physical shortcomings, I was temporarily confined to yoga pants and T-shirts, so I felt at a distinct disadvantage and was wickedly gratified when our dog jumped up at her one snowy day and left paw prints on her white wool coat.

Our first exchange was not promising. 'I would recommend a ceiling-track hoist to be installed in the living room,' she began.

'Why?' I asked. 'That would mean we could only use it downstairs: David needs help lifting Cara in and out of bed and the bath upstairs. In any case, I'm expecting another baby, so wouldn't that be a safety hazard once it starts to move around?'

'Well, most people with other children seem to manage,' she sniffed. 'Perhaps we could install a lift in the corner of your living room and a hoist upstairs.'

'We had thought of building an extension on the side of the house,' I said, innocent at that time of the implications of what I was saying. 'Couldn't you perhaps put something on that – as well as being safer for our other child – would actually enhance the house?'

I had voiced the unthinkable. Not only had I asked for an extension, when it was their policy not to build them at all, but I had actually dared to imagine that what they did might improve things for us. Oliver Twist asking for more could not have made a greater negative impact.

'We don't feel that that's fair,' she said, rather sanctimoniously. 'We only have a limited amount of money and we have to ensure that everyone gets the same, so that everyone's equal.'

I struggled with this. 'But Cara is completely disabled, so she *isn't* really "equal" to the majority of disabled children.'

I showed her around the house. She did no measuring at all. After she had gone, I rang David in tears and asked him to have a word. He called back later, saying that she was going to make another visit with a building surveyor.

This she duly did and told us that she would be recommending making Cara live downstairs, adapting the garage for her use and installing a shower. I watched in silence as the surveyor measured up.

Our lives had already been invaded by the education department; now the OT and building services departments were apparently preparing to invade our house too. In no area of our existence were we able to take time out from being parents of a severely disabled child, because now even our family home, it appeared, was going to be transformed into a makeshift care home. Our family life, and the rights of our other daughter, were of no consequence; they were going to do what they thought was appropriate for Cara alone, tick the boxes and walk away.

At the end of the measuring up, David asked the surveyor how much the alterations would cost.

'Oh, I would estimate about £10,000.'

'And how much of that would you meet?'

'Well, at present, you have been assessed as having an entitlement to a nil grant.'

David drew a deep breath. 'OK, thanks, but no thanks. We'll wait for the abolition of the means test and see what happens then.'

The surveyor received this piece of information with equanimity. Not so the occupational therapist, who looked offended but stayed silent. I went back inside, while David chatted to her about a portable hoist, which was the only thing he was currently prepared to accept.

At the time, we weren't aware that we had good reasons for refusing what they were proposing. All I had were my gut instincts as a mother that the adaptations wouldn't meet Cara's needs for very long, if at all, and that they would fruitlessly wreck our home. I think also that at the beginning we simply trusted people who claimed that they knew what was best for Cara, for several reasons: first, we had no knowledge of the field ourselves; second, we had argued with the LEA and it was getting us nowhere except into more arguments; and third, we could not face the prospect of yet another prolonged fight running concurrently with the dispute we were already having.

During that year, we exchanged letters with the OT department. We refused the garage conversion on the basis that it denied Cara access to half the house, and her paediatrician thought it inadvisable for Cara to be so far away from us when she suffered from epilepsy. We also questioned whether or not the garage, once all the equipment was installed, would accommodate Cara when she had undergone a few more years of growth. The OT department did not budge, and the process stretched to a whole year.

The problem was at least temporarily solved when we failed to get Cara to Northern Counties the following December. We had every intention of finding another authority with better prospects for her education than Sunderland and so we suspended our relationship with the OT department. Eventually, however, we were advised that the other authorities were not significantly better and that we would do well to stay put and complete the fight where we had begun it. So once again, David called the OT department to ask for a visit, and the whole process recommenced. Those last two years of Cara's life were to be the hardest and most gruelling times we had ever experienced.

# 10  Unless the Lord Builds the House

We had discovered a new coffee shop at the old harbour at Seaham, situated right on the seafront, which served wonderful food and coffee and was full of quirky ornaments and homewares. It became a brief haven for us; almost every Saturday or Sunday, we would escape with the children to have lunch and breathe the fresh air. David would feed Cara soup and I would feed Charis her jar of baby food and whatever bits of my own lunch I could persuade her to eat. I would wander through the shop, looking at the vintage prints and crockery, perhaps subconsciously referring back to my own childhood when life was rather simpler. We would drink coffee – and then we would get back to whatever issue we were dealing with in regard to Cara, talking around it and through it yet again, until lunchtime was over and it had once again been the main topic of conversation. After that, we would go and stare at the sea, which briefly calmed me and gave me a sense of perspective about what was happening.

The law course gave me hope that, at some point, we would get for Cara the education she needed. But having a new problem in the picture was not something we had anticipated. We really believed that Northern Counties would make a difference to Cara, and even if we had wanted to give up, we now had such a reputation with the LEA that I think it was unlikely we could have withdrawn. But another fight in addition, requiring the same amount of painstaking effort, all the while racing to get things sorted before Cara grew too big – that was too much for us.

I wish that I could say that I had an abiding sense of the Lord's presence, but at this time the struggle to stay afloat had become so acute, and we had both become so driven, that willpower alone seemed to be keeping us going. I barely managed to concentrate on God for more than a few minutes at a time, because all the while my mind would be turning over the issues, worrying at them like a bulldog. The support given to us by our groups was what we needed, and no-one at church could have done any more for us than they did. Equally, I think that we did as much as we could in turning up at church, house group and small group, and trying to stay in a place where God could reach us; I think it helped to keep us stable and sane, but it couldn't change our situation.

It underlined for me yet again the importance of habit in the practice of faith, regardless of how one feels – that it is important to persevere in hard times. Staying within a worshipping community, praying, studying Scripture, even making in our heads the most insignificant acts of trust and faith in God, I believe, held things together for us as individuals and as a couple.

I was acutely aware that God did not 'have' to intervene and make everything all right for us. Bonhoeffer's words come to mind: 'When Christ calls a man, he bids him come and die.'[1] God has not promised to make our lives easy. He sometimes allows us to go through exactly the same difficulties as those outside the kingdom, in part so that we can offer Christ's comfort from the heart to those in the same circumstances, and in part so that we can continue to be witnesses for his way of doing things where it is most needed.

The second letter to the Corinthians talks about creation 'groaning' and 'travailing' like a woman in labour until God's purposes are finally achieved and it is fully renewed; God's kingdom is both now, and not yet, and sometimes while it is being brought in, Christians must suffer as the result of human wrongdoing just the same as everyone else. That does not mean that God is not ultimately in control, or that he does not suffer with us, but that we are part of a much greater vision of love and truth that we are not always, in this life at any rate, equipped to understand. My great solace at this time was to know that there is no such thing, in Christ, as meaningless suffering. And I knew that, in the words of Mother Julian of Norwich, 'Love was his meaning.'[2]

We ourselves had undergone a radical change. The circumstances brought out both the best and the worst in us: sometimes we were good, passionately committed Christians with a level of awareness of injustice and a capacity to endure that was well beyond that of many people, but we were also angry, cynical, ideological zealots. Proverbs 17:3 talks about gold being tried in the furnace (whereby the ore is heated and reheated seven times, and the impurities are burned away until, at last, the goldsmith can see his face in it). We showed up a lot of impurities as we underwent our respective furnaces. But, by God's grace, and perhaps by our own bloody-mindedness, we hung on.

In the earlier days of our fight, I had read stories and watched films about people succeeding against the odds, filling my inner landscape with fiction and non-fiction about the last world war, about the civil rights movement, and courtroom dramas with unpredictable positive outcomes. Stories have always been important to me and they became a lifeline, offering hope and lifting my morale.

But now I began to be drawn to books and films that were less upbeat, and gradually, over time, I started to read stories of people like Dietrich Bonhoeffer, St Edmund Campion, the

Anglican Reformation martyrs, people who had challenged authority and lost, finding strength in their responses to the awareness that if they held to their convictions, the ultimate sacrifice would be required. My subconscious and my imagination were perhaps telling me that maybe the outcome wouldn't be what we hoped for; more superficially, I was reminded that things could be a lot worse, and my resolve to keep on fighting, whatever it took, remained strong in spite of everything. I think some of it was just native stubbornness, but some of it also was a dawning awareness that there were important principles at stake here: if God was allowing this, then there was a deeper purpose at work and we had to carry it through, no matter the cost to ourselves.

Cara now had a new social worker; Rebecca had been replaced by Allie, a woman of about my own age. Unfortunately for us, she did not have the flair that Rebecca had possessed. Meeting her for the first time was a depressing experience, because she gave the impression that her priorities would be paperwork and cost-cutting, which grated on us. Early on, she proposed to remove one of our carers, a move which was halted by a note from my doctor about my back problems. After that, we didn't feel we could altogether trust her.

In June, we were given our new OT assessment and a new member of staff, Louise. She only worked part-time, but we were considerably happier both with her attitude and with the level of her expertise and experience.

She told us that the idea to convert the garage by fitting a shower would not work, because Cara did not have the required muscle capability to sit in a shower chair. She would need a full-size bath, with a hoist and a specially fitted bath mattress. She measured our main bathroom fully and, contrary to previous advice, told us that it was too small to accommodate the kind of lifting equipment that would be needed for Cara. What was required was a larger bath that was accessible on four sides, with a cradle-hoist. We digested this slowly, thinking what a waste of money it would have been if we had agreed to the garage conversion.

At a later date, she brought a sales representative for a lift company to assess the house. The rep measured up and told us that if a lift was installed in the dining room, the room could not be used for anything else because of the clearance needed for the door and the wheelchair. He also told us that Cara's bedroom was too small to accommodate a lift and that the same was true of Charis's bedroom. He recommended some form of extension.

The means test had been abolished the previous December, so we now had a case for an extension proposal. Our solution was simple: outside our house was an area to the side of the garage, which I think had been at some point earmarked for a second garage. There was space to build a two-storey extension on to the house that could accommodate Cara with an upstairs bedroom, an adapted bathroom accessible by lift, and an equipment store plus playroom, for her entire life, no matter how tall she grew.

We would need far less help from social services, because if we were given the right equipment, we could take care of her ourselves, or we could pay a nurse if I wanted to work. However, we could not afford to do this without a Disabled Facilities Grant from the local authority, and the grant depended on an assessment by an occupational therapist.

Therein lay the difficulty for us, because the OT department was only prepared to give us money for the original assessment, even though Louise had subsequently proved that it was not the correct solution for Cara. (I must add here that there was a substantial amount of government money available in a special fund, so the council would not have been out of pocket if they had given Cara what she needed.)

So there we were, with letters and suggestions batting back and forth between us and the OT department, and again, getting nowhere. They kept sending out officials to do measuring and assessment, one after the other (I think that in total we had more than ten people turn up at our house), but nothing ever came of it. This state of affairs lasted for seven months.

During the summer holiday in 2006, I got the result of my paralegal course assessment: I had achieved a distinction, which I was very happy with. No sooner had this happened than I was plunged into a frenzy of letter writing. One of my letters was written to our local Member of Parliament. We had a telephone call from him within days, in which he expressed honest disgust at the difficulties we were having. He said that he would contact the chief executive of the city council immediately on our behalf and see what could be done to progress things as quickly as possible.

Within a couple of weeks, we had a communication from the OT department offering us a grant of £25,000, the maximum mandatory grant possible at that time. We breathed again, but only for a while, because we knew that this would not be enough.

In our hallway is a small sampler, worked in cross-stitch, a National Trust embroidery kit that I once bought when I wanted to do something creative. One night in 2003, after David had gone to bed, I had decided to adapt the design slightly to put in a Bible verse:

Unless the LORD builds the house,
   its builders labour in vain.
(Psalm 127:1)

Like many Bible verses, this can have a variety of applications, but it had seemed to fit our situation well when I added it to the sampler, back in 2003. It reminded us that all of our efforts will come to nothing unless we seek to line up with God's plans first and continue to keep reviewing them so that they remain in line with what he wants. Well, here we were, approaching four years later, trying our utmost to line up with God's plans for Cara to have a future, but being thwarted at every turn by those with the power, who seemed unwilling to concede even the slightest detail of what we believed was right for her.

I felt the verse became a prophecy for the council. They had insisted on having her in Coquet Vale, and the result was – absolutely nothing. Those who worked there with Cara laboured in vain. She was slipping backwards, catching more illnesses, becoming more withdrawn at home. This was also true of the OT department, who spent an enormous amount of time and energy drawing up proposals that, because of some obvious flaw, turned out to be completely unworkable.

We were told to draw up some plans ourselves to give them some idea of what we thought was suitable. Naively we believed that this might help, so we contacted a builder to come and talk to us, both about our proposals and about the sketch-plans drawn up by the building surveyor.

He was a down-to-earth, practical man. He studied the OT plans carefully.

'I can't see why they're suggesting these,' he said. 'Even with the cost of all the extra equipment, your solution is the cheapest. And if you did what they want, you'd have all the expense of putting it to rights if you ever needed to leave. What you need to do now is get an architect to look at it and draw up some plans. I usually work with this guy; I think he could help you.'

We duly contacted the architect. He was a solidly built Scot, with the air of an elder statesman and a quiet voice, who very clearly knew what he was talking about. He rejected the council's first two solutions out of hand, but after careful measuring, produced a beautiful set of plans for building on the left side of the house, for which we paid.

We duly submitted the plans and waited for a response. The next news we had, about a fortnight later, was a communication from the building surveyor in charge of our case, drawing attention to a number of what he saw as 'difficulties' with the plans.

We immediately telephoned the architect, who spoke to David at work, struggling to control his irritation. 'What's all this about underpinning the foundations? The house is built on bedrock.'

'Oh, he based that on the fact that he did some work further down the street,' David said.

'And he's saying that the lift is going to be too small. Well, having measured your daughter's wheelchair, I know he's wrong about that too – who is he, anyway?'

After a number of further weeks had elapsed, the OT department agreed to meet with us and with the architect. By this time, matters were becoming critical in terms of David lifting Cara. She was now too heavy for him to lift in and out of the bath, and after one awful incident, when he dropped her and her face went under the water, he telephoned the social worker and said that he couldn't do it any more. She was eventually able to arrange for Cara to have showers at school as a temporary measure twice a week. Unfortunately, at weekends, and in the evenings, we were still faced with the same problem.

At this point Cara was taking regular doses of laxatives; because of her size and relative immobility, her bowels had become very sluggish. Typically what would happen would be that she would fail to open her bowels for several days, and become pale and sickly; we would call the hospital and would be advised to increase the laxative powder she was taking. Then, we would have an explosion – this would usually mean that the clothes she was wearing would have to be binned, and with the aid of bowls of water and baby wipes, we would have to somehow clean her up. A further complication was that as far as she was concerned, diarrhoea was just another texture to play with, so one of us would have to literally hold her arms out of the way while we cleaned her on her exercise mat, which would then have to be washed and sprayed down with disinfectant.

This would have been easy if she had been the same physical size as the baby she was developmentally, but she was very tall and long-limbed. In her last year and a half, she had started puberty, so we had a child with tiny, budding breasts as well, and that made it even more undignified and degrading for her.

If we had been willing to opt for one of the solutions the OT department had come up with, would it really have made any difference? Given the signs that the building surveyor seemed to be struggling with such a big project, and the disagreements surrounding the OT assessments, I think we would probably have ended up with a so-called solution that wouldn't have met Cara's needs, and that in itself could well have been a source of building problems – which we would have had to pay to have rectified. With this in our heads, therefore, we struggled grimly on.

Finally, because Cara had now reached the statutory age of eight, she was legally entitled to respite care. The Beachy Head Centre in Sunderland was the one bright spot at that time in her life; purpose-built, state-of-the-art, it offered everything we wanted for her. There was a limit on the number of visits, but she obviously enjoyed her weekends there. I particularly loved the bright, light-filled decoration of the bedrooms and the big orthopaedic beds with their vibrantly patterned duvet covers. At home, she was still sleeping in her old child's bed, and we had been holding off decorating her room for the last couple of years because we had been expecting a decision about the extension. And despite the urgency that was obvious to anyone directly involved with Cara, the council seemed to be in no great hurry to resolve the situation.

I went into hospital at the beginning of April 2007; I had been granted a breast reduction operation on the NHS because I had been experiencing back and neck problems; it was a major operation and I was slow to recover. We had another meeting with the OT department and with the surveyor a fortnight afterwards, but I had to cry off. David fielded it on his own. The OT service manager as good as blamed us for the fact that the situation was no nearer a solution. 'It's only because of your tenacity that we are still here,' she said.

Cara was booked into respite for five days in May to allow us to go on holiday for the first time in about six years. We had booked a few days in Prague, but the day before we were due to go, I didn't feel I could cope. We had to cancel, and instead of an exotic trip abroad, we had a few quiet days in Norfolk. We had trips to Sandringham, Hunstanton and Wells-next-the-Sea, and strolled on shingle beaches, making the most of unseasonably warm weather. I knew that if I was to be of any use at all, I had to recover, so I made the most of the holiday, tucking into fried breakfasts and sitting in the sun.

When we got back, another meeting was arranged at our house with the building surveyor, the architect, and now the complaints officer, to try to discuss some of the issues that the council had with our design.

The architect was superb. Without even trying, and in his customary careful, measured tones, he explained the flaws in the surveyor's objections, the coup de grâce coming when Cara arrived home from school, and we were able to measure her wheelchair and prove that the objection to the size of the lift had been completely unfounded. The meeting ended with a cautious agreement for our solution to be costed.

Our second appeal to the MP, over the need for extra money to be provided, had resulted in an intervention by the head of adult services, who had instigated a Stage 3 Complaint.[3] By this time, I had while surfing the Internet one night come across what is known colloquially as the Bristol Report, a very useful document emanating from the Office of the Deputy Prime Minister.

It explored the issues surrounding the assessment for and funding of the Disabled Facilities Grant. It addressed all the problems we had experienced: the need for access to all areas of the house for a disabled person, consideration of the needs of the rest of the family including siblings, and funding issues. Some councils, for example, had introduced low-interest loan schemes and contracts specifying a time limit for repayment. However, our OT department claimed to be unaware of the report and later based most of their argument on the fact that it was not yet legislation, so they did not have to comply with it.

David had been experiencing acute back pain, and on visiting the doctor, was told that he should not be lifting Cara at all. The problem had now become so serious that if the OT department did not move quickly, Cara would have to go into residential care while it was being sorted out, which would mean that social services would have to foot the considerable bill. In reality, this was very much a last-resort solution for us, and we hoped and expected that it would not have to happen. Allie, in a panic, spoke to her senior manager, who decided, along with everyone else, to pay us a visit.

She said she had been given the impression that we were hard-bitten opportunists, but left us with a very different view after looking at our house, at the various proposals the OT department had offered, and talking to us at length about how we felt the proposals would affect Cara and the rest of the family. She said that she would not have liked to have lived in what the OT department wanted to give us and she fully entered into the concerns we had for Charis, not just in terms of her immediate physical safety, but also with regard to her future opportunities to have a reasonable life as Cara's sister. She left promising to do her best to help us, but it seemed that even she would not stick her neck out.

The complaints procedure went ahead with a visit from the complaints officer and a pleasant Dutch lady who had been brought in as an impartial observer. The officer, a cordial, white-haired Yorkshireman, listened attentively, smiling and nodding at all the right moments, but failed to identify our main issues in his preliminary report. The Dutch lady struggled to understand exactly what was being said and had only a limited understanding of legislation. I repeated everything I had said before and hoped for the best.

When we read the preliminary report, we decided to let it be submitted on the basis that the officer had privately indicated to David in a telephone conversation that he hoped to sort things out for us quickly. We had come to realize that 'quickly' was a fairly relative term; even if we succeeded, it would take a minimum of twelve additional weeks for the plans to go through the planning department, about six weeks for the proposed builders to tender their contracts, and then about two months for it to be built.

Two weeks later, our hopes were shattered again. The building surveyor decided to cost the plans at £45,000, a figure that no-one had even mentioned before, above the threshold of money that the council could write off and far more than we could afford to pay. Worse, he even suggested that the cost might go up to £65,000 or higher. We could not make any plans to meet the extra amount of money without knowing how much the maximum amount was going to be. We had been out-manoeuvred.

We were determined to fight on, because now we had no choice. However, Cara's situation was becoming harder and harder – and the long-term consequences of the council's decision were ones that none of us had any way of foreseeing.

# 11  Business as Usual

At Coquet Vale, Cara had now changed classes. We continued to have the glitches that we had come to expect. It had been identified that Cara needed to have a switch fitted to her wheelchair so that she could be encouraged to respond by using it, as part of her communication programme, but the time went on and nothing happened; it was finally scheduled for November 2006, about nine months after it had first been mooted, but Cara happened to be off school when the appropriate personnel finally came to do the assessment. It was then postponed until the following term.

There was still no occupational therapist, though we were assured that one would be starting after half-term. I learned to write up my evidence, write the letters, make the phone calls and leave it behind. At this point, I couldn't even contemplate what this neglect was doing to Cara, because it would have disabled me completely.

The poor levels of organization permeated every level of life at the school. The practice was to change children's incontinence pads twice a day, but Cara often came home either with her pad leaking, or in school trousers because she had been allowed to get wet or dirty. I suggested to her class teacher that they might change her three times a day instead.

I dislike the morbid levels of sentimentality that are often expressed in relation to many disabled children. Phrases like 'a little angel', 'her smile lights up the room' and 'what a little treasure' are often applied to children with severely limited capabilities of whom nothing is expected, other than that they will lie in a chair or a bed for all of their usually short lives and look as decorative as they can be made to. Such sentimentality somehow places these children in a different category of life from the rest of us, as if they were somehow not human. This in turn makes it subtly easier for people to believe that these children do not require the same rights as other, able-bodied people – such as effective therapy programmes or an appropriate education. I also wonder what happens when some of these little angels grow up and are a lot more expensive to take care of, and not so obviously attractive to casual, uninvolved observers.

When people are emoting, said Alfred Hitchcock, they are not thinking and analysing – and in the current climate, creative thinking and analysing, followed up with effective practical action, are what these children need most of all. The phrases I mention above were heard a lot at Coquet Vale, and they even entered Cara's annual review documents. Interestingly, I never heard anyone talk this way at Northern Counties, perhaps because they really saw the children as just that: individual children who needed vast amounts of help, but not, thank God, 'little angels' with 'lovely smiles'!

At the end of the autumn term in 2006, we had Cara's annual review with the LEA. We consulted with a solicitor and were instructed not only to ask the appropriate questions, but also to make extensive notes so that nothing could be left out of the official minutes. If we could provide enough evidence, then Cara's statement would have to be changed to accommodate new information. And if the local authority changed her statement, then we might just get another tribunal, which would allow us to demand a school change. In any case, the Education Act and the Code of Practice both said that if parents were dissatisfied with the school to which the child had been sent after tribunal, they could after a year demand that the child was moved to another state school, even one outside the authority.

A useful piece of information came from the new educational psychologist, who confirmed that Cara was not going to make progress at present with the use of Makaton signing. We had tried to tell Cara's teachers that her eyesight wasn't good enough to make signing worthwhile, but the class teacher and the deputy head had continued with it. However, the educational psychologist said that Cara was barely able to cope with objects of reference, such as nappies to indicate toileting needs, and spoons to indicate dinner, and that symbolic communication of any kind was currently too advanced for her.

David managed to engineer a video assessment for Cara by the senior speech therapist, to take place in January, to assess whether or not she performed better when given one-to-one help. In the event, this was proven on the video beyond any shadow of doubt, but even with this, the school claimed that they did this kind of thing with Cara anyway – of course we had no way of knowing if this happened consistently.

Cara had been assessed using PIVATS, one of the programmes used to assess special needs children who performed at a certain basic level. But Cara did not reach even this basic level and therefore, we felt, could not have her abilities accurately assessed by it. We raised the question of whether or not it was appropriate to assess Cara this way. No agreement was reached on this question, but PIVATS was apparently the only available assessment method for special needs children in Sunderland.

I wrote my own set of minutes and managed to have them accepted alongside the official ones, which, written by the school secretary, did not reflect any of the differences of opinion. We waited for a response. Nothing. So finally, at the end of January, I wrote to the SEN Head and said that since it was clear that no-one was going to support our requests for a statement change, we were invoking our right under the Education Act to have Cara moved to a different school, out of the authority.

Meanwhile, our other complaint about the email had finally borne some fruit. Once the council realized that we were going to continue to ask questions until something was done, they offered us mediation in the hope of finding a way forward. We agreed, because by this time we knew that it was probably the best we were going to get.

As I had before, I spent the summer term looking for a school that would be able to take Cara. I rang up the various local authorities that surrounded Sunderland asking for lists of schools to call. One authority turned us down flat, even though legally they were not supposed to, because they said that their schools were already oversubscribed. That left us with Durham and South Tyneside, both of which were near enough to us for Cara to be able to go to school without us having to move.

The only school that was a possibility for Cara in Durham was the exotically named Valparaiso School, at Consett. So one sunny morning, while Charis was with her minder, I boarded the bus to Consett to have a look round and a chat with staff.

I was expecting something that looked like a rundown seaside boarding house, but I was pleasantly surprised by the building, which was new. It had good hydrotherapy facilities and a busy, purposive atmosphere. It took children until they were eighteen, and although it did have some disruptive pupils, it also had an isolation unit. The classes were small, and I was able to chat to a classroom assistant whose son attended the school. The deputy head seemed very happy at the idea of taking Cara.

But of course, I should have known after all this time that nothing was going to be straightforward. Over the ensuing weeks, the Durham SEN department at the council steadfastly maintained that there was no place for Cara and that it was impossible for her to go there. According to the Education Act, as long as the school was willing to have her and as long as her needs fitted the school's designation, Cara was entitled to attend, but the authority still refused.

We couldn't even summon up the energy to fight this strategy; we just moved on to the next school, Walford Avenue in South Shields. It was less well equipped, but we liked the head teacher, and the school felt very similar to our first impressions of Sarah Millman, with its pleasant, committed staff. The authority was also due for a restructure and we thought that that might work in our favour at Cara's statutory reassessment in two years' time. Since we had already made our feelings about Sunderland clear, then if her needs were not met at Walford Avenue, it would strengthen our case to have her moved to Northern Counties.

So we learned another lesson about special needs education; all parents theoretically have a choice of school out of the authority if their child's needs are not met within it – but in our experience, this 'choice' is as illusory as the one that says we have a choice of school within the authority. All LEAs struggle to meet the needs of their own children, and none wants to take on a child from somewhere else; in fact, as we discovered, there can be considerable hostility towards LEAs who try to push their children out of area. We made the decision to settle for the moment, because we needed the break from all the conflict, and in that respect, Walford Avenue was actually a reasonable solution for everyone.

The mediator came to our house in the summer term, a thin, nervous-looking little man trying to be nice, but not really able to deal with the kind of emotions we had experienced over the years. He listened carefully to our case, thanked me for being so honest, as if he was giving me counselling rather than trying to sort out a legal matter, and scheduled a meeting for the following month at which we could discuss our differences with the SEN Head and the statement writer.

The mediation meeting was mostly a damp squib, because we had already decided on our course of action. When the meeting took place, we had not yet visited Walford Avenue, but the outcome was predetermined by the law, and the Sunderland SEN Head was obliged to do the work on our behalf to try to find a place for Cara. So after seven long years, we had a stalemate: they had not got exactly what they wanted, but then, neither had we. It was an unsatisfactory truce in this long and weary fight.

The mediator tried to keep things pleasant and we did arrive at an agreement, which from his point of view, I suppose, was some level of success. The reality was, however, that he was only needed to draw up the agreement and make it official. The SEN Head now had to find Cara a place in another state special school outside the authority, or, as he was aware, our next course of action would be to keep Cara at home and petition for her to go to Northern Counties instead.

The issue of Cara's accommodation and homecare was about to hit us again. Social services, following the visit by the senior social worker, had finally ordered a mandatory Core Assessment, an all-round appraisal of every aspect of Cara's life in an attempt to obtain extra funding for the extension from the social services budget.

Cara's summer holidays started with a sense of hope; at least she would not return to Coquet Vale in the autumn term, which was some success given the difficulties we had had. Summer holidays were always fraught with a certain amount of difficulty for us, however, and more especially now that we had Charis, because I could not go out unless we had someone to stay with Cara. Charis was too small to walk by herself, and I could not manage Cara's wheelchair as well; in fact, even if we had not had Charis, I would have found it hard to push Cara on and off buses, because she was now very tall and too heavy for me.

In the first summer after Charis was born, social services had arranged for one of her helpers to take Cara out for two afternoons each week. That had been refused us this year, so my mother came to sit with Cara while I took Charis out in her buggy. It was arranged for Cara to attend the Coquet Vale play scheme, which we wanted only because it was the sole holiday provision for her, but, said our social worker, we would have to make arrangements for transport ourselves. So, again, the wearingly familiar struggles about the details of provision began.

The logistics of arranging something were so difficult that David, after a lot of arguing, ended up being able only to get transport for the first week and had to take time off work so that he could take Cara to the play scheme himself.

As school was now out, Cara could no longer have showers, so we tried to organize something for her with social services. Allie's solution was for David to undergo a training course at the Beachy Head Centre and take her for a pre-arranged bath during the day. Unfortunately, even if he had been able to take the additional time off work, by the time he had completed the course the holiday would have been nearly over.

We were not looking forward to the Core Assessment interviews for the extension funding, and when Allie arrived at the house to do mine, I was nervous and expecting some kind of confrontation. But nothing had prepared me for the body blow that followed.

I had filled in a sheet for inclusion, and first of all Allie took issue with me because, after the initial use of Cara's name, I had referred to her as 'she'. I hadn't thought twice about it, but Allie saw some sinister psychological significance, because, she said, it indicated to her that I was a distant parent. While I was still digesting this, worse was to follow.

'You see, Rhona, I get the impression that you resent Cara and the impact she's made on your life.'

I started to laugh. When I spoke, I said quietly, 'You're mistaken. I resent the bureaucracy that makes all our lives so difficult, but never Cara. If I resented Cara, why would I have given my job up to look after her?'

She didn't answer this but continued. 'And you see, Rhona, a number of people have heard you talking about putting Cara into care in front of her; that's – well, it's emotional abuse, Rhona, and I must ask you please not to do it.'

This was the worst accusation yet. We had been called many things, but 'abusive' had never before been included. I briefly thought of the children I had seen being manhandled, screamed at and sworn at by stressed-out mothers. Cara had never had such treatment.

I got up and walked across the room, because my first impulse was to order her to leave, but the self-control that had been developed over years warned me to finish the interview.

'That is outrageous,' I said, speaking quickly. 'And if you intend to put that in your report, then I can promise you, you will be getting a letter from our solicitor. Cara can't understand what we are saying – do you seriously imagine that we would say it in front of her if she knew what we were talking about?'

'We don't know what Cara can understand,' she said self-righteously.

I do, I thought. According to her educational psychologist and the senior speech therapist, she couldn't understand speech at all, so abstract concepts like 'in care' wouldn't have any impact whatsoever. Why didn't Allie know that?

'I have to think about Cara,' she said. 'She is my priority in this.'

I looked at her in surprise. And you think she isn't ours? I wanted to say.

I didn't bother to explain. 'How much more of this is there to do?' I asked curtly, sitting down again on the sofa. 'Because I'd like to get it over with as quickly as possible.'

I answered the rest of her questions as briefly as I could, and showed her out. I brooded and fretted all weekend about it, but even worse was to follow when the draft assessment arrived on the following Thursday. I opened it myself and read it in mounting horror.

Sure enough, I came over as a remote, distant parent, who was perceived as being uninvolved with Cara at an emotional level. With regard to school, Allie said that Cara was perfectly happy at Coquet Vale and would settle down if we would just stop trying to move her around. On the question of the extension, she sided with the authority. Perhaps the easiest way around a problem that was too complex was for her to place all the blame on us as difficult parents, and on me in particular as a mother, in a report characterized by a limited understanding of the facts and by complete support of the local authority's view on every aspect of Cara's life.

When David met me at home, I was in tears. I sat down at the computer after dinner and began to go through the assessment, page by page. I corrected her errors, set the record factually straight about school and the extension, and ended by writing that Allie seemed unreasonably resistant to considering Cara's situation within the family.

It seems now, considered superficially, to be a very un-Christian response. But it felt then that the only right thing to do was to fight back. If I had allowed the report to be submitted unchallenged, it could have caused damaging repercussions for us, and even if I had not been angry, I don't think my reply to it would have been substantially different. It was impossible for me to write other than directly in response to what felt like a deliberate personal attack, designed to push us into a corner.

In the days following, I would get up in the mornings and go through my normal routines like a sleepwalker, trying hard not to think about the horrors that might descend on us during the day. Doing the practical things helped: the washing, the ironing, the dusting and vacuuming. All my energies were now taken up simply with survival. Allie's intervention had been meant to move the situation forward, but instead, we felt more isolated than ever.

We took out our pain on each other, David and I, having lots of stupid rows about nothing, but there was never any 'abuse', verbal or otherwise, of our children, and they were both well cared for. The most ironic aspect of this standoff between us and the council is that the family pressures that nearly pushed us over the edge were almost entirely caused by our interaction with them, by the difficulties and disagreements we experienced in having our situation assessed correctly, and by our deep frustration that Cara's needs seemed to be a low priority by comparison to budgetary requirements.

I don't know how long this would have gone on – probably until one or other of us became too ill to cope. I prayed and prayed for God to intervene, but no-one was listening to him, least of all our tormentors. Then we awoke one Thursday morning to find Cara in a deep seizure, and, however hard it seems, I think that in the end he answered our prayers in the only way he was allowed to: in his mysterious and infinite mercy, he took Cara to be with him.

## 12  Make Way

The following days blur into each other; I was calm, but I was numb, and lots of things failed to make much of an impression. The sense that I was walking in a different dimension, as I had during those last days in hospital when the veil between heaven and earth seemed to be very thin and I knew exactly what to do, continued; like Peter on the mountain at the Transfiguration, I, very strangely, wished that I could have stayed there for ever because of the sense of the Lord directing my steps and walking with me. But inevitably, the world came back, and it came back straight away.

After a long sleep, we got up the following day and decided to go for a drive, because we did not at that time want to deal with telephone calls and visitors. We ended up at the Alnwick Garden, but because we had the dog with us, we couldn't go in. We slowly drove home again, remembering the time after Cara's diagnosis when we had escaped in the same way, driving away, not answering the telephone, to be alone with our pain.

We had got back at about teatime when the doorbell rang, and I opened the door to a very young, pleasant-faced policeman. He said that he had come to deal with some formalities, and he came in and sat down.

'There are just a few questions I need to ask about your daughter's death,' he began.

I felt a surge of pure horror. 'You don't think we had anything to do with it, do you?' I gasped.

He smiled, and took pains to reassure me that this was a routine procedure in the event of an unexpected death and that everyone who had been involved in Cara's last days would be questioned in the same way, including the care-workers. We had already been forewarned by the senior consultant at the hospital the previous day that there would have to be a post-mortem, because there was no clear-cut reason why Cara, at only nine years of age and with no history of heart problems, should have gone into cardiac arrest. Apparently what we said was satisfactory, because he went away and didn't come back.

We continued to move through the week. The funeral was going to be delayed because of the post-mortem, so that peculiar time between a death and a funeral was going to be prolonged for us, and it wasn't until the following week that we received permission to arrange the funeral for the week after. So in the end we had a time together as a small family that was strangely like a holiday. Often, we took Charis and the dog to Saltwell Park in Gateshead, where we met my mother and walked and talked in the sun, and drank coffee on the terrace of Saltwell Towers. The weather was beautiful, and it was as if we were being taken care of and blessed even by that.

The cards and the telephone calls poured in. The house was filled with flowers, and our house group brought food so that we had minimal cooking to do. I remember the time as an eternity, but in a good way, as if Cara's gentle presence had not quite left us but was continuing to work for good in our lives, and the sense of God's overshadowing and comfort met us in everything. We had been made privy to the secret places of the Most High in the life that we had lived with

Cara; suffering with her and for her had inevitably given us a different and deepened understanding of the problem of pain, and now we were abiding in the shadow of the Almighty, resting and being made whole even in our grief and loss.

There was never any sense for us that Cara was not in existence any more; rather, the feeling increased that she was living a much fuller and richer life elsewhere, and that we had not really lost her. I missed, as any mother would, the touch of her always-questing slim brown hands, the smell of her hair, the heavy dark lashes, the physical presence that latterly had come to look so much like me and my family – but the essence of Cara, the gentle spirit that had inhabited her impaired body, there was no sense at all that that had gone. It was as if we lost her and gained her at the same time, because we knew that she was finally free to be the child she should have been, no longer at the mercy of appliances and drugs, but released into real life at last. Eternity for her wouldn't be eternal rest, I thought; it would be eternal movement and play and doing all the things she couldn't do while she was here. We mourned for her and we were glad for her. I had said when she was dying that death wasn't final; I knew the emotional reality of that, and I still do.

We contacted the undertaker, the one who had always done my family's funerals, and explained the situation regarding the inquest. He was extremely good – sensitive, compassionate and at the same time very professional indeed.

The clergy at the church were temporarily headed up by the Reverend Dr Rosalyn Murphy, the curate, an attractive African-American lady with a vivacious personality, a creative dress sense (she is the only woman I have seen to date who manages to make a clerical shirt look stylish) and a strongly traditional and extrovert faith. When we arrived at the church to discuss the funeral arrangements, we felt that we were in safe hands, because our views on what we wanted – a celebration of Cara's life, an affirmation of her eternal destination and an overall message of hope – meshed perfectly with the approach she wanted to take. We talked together a lot about the problems we had had during Cara's life, and one of the comments she made was that perhaps God had finally intervened in the only way he could to end Cara's difficulties and our suffering, in view of how implacable the system had been and how resistant to any kind of civilized and creative solution.

Rosalyn told us that she usually felt mystified by the average British attitude to church funerals: abject silent misery, minimal preaching and a general sense of embarrassed heaviness from which everyone escapes in relief to get drunk and forget. We were absolutely determined, even in our pain, that Cara would have the best that we could manage, a traditionally Christian funeral that talked honestly and positively about eternal life and its meaning, and didn't pander to the buttoned-up good taste of the average send-off. In some sense, we were free to do that, because the funeral of someone like Cara couldn't really fit into the same mould as the funeral of an older person who had been able to live a normal life.

We had, however, lots of people to consider. We knew that, whether we wanted it or not, Cara's funeral was going to be very public indeed and that we had to abide by some of the conventions. David and I bought new clothes, appropriately black and grey, and issued a general ban on flowers, asking instead that donations be given to a children's hospice fund in Sunderland. However, we ordered a beautiful waterfall of flowers to drape over the coffin, which on the day looked simple and effective by itself.

We chose the readings with care, concentrating on the idea of healing – Jairus's daughter, the healing of the man born blind 'so that the work of God might be displayed in his life' (John 9:3) – but beginning with the beautiful words from Ecclesiastes that place God squarely in charge of shaping and refining everything that happens:

There is a time for everything,
and a season for every activity under heaven.
(Ecclesiastes 3:1)

I chose this passage because I wanted to underline the point that we didn't feel that Cara's death was just a meaningless, random tragedy, but the final act in a life that in God's eyes had fulfilled its purpose and that he was now reclaiming. We couldn't have read, but in the end, Alex from our house group, Kathryn from my small group, and Janet our childminder, who had been through so much with us, agreed to do the readings for us.

Because Cara had loved music so much, we chose some jazz saxophone pieces, one by Coleman Hawkins to play as the mourners gathered and one by Dexter Gordon to accompany a video montage of Cara that David assembled from footage that we had taken over the years, ending with her playing with a keyboard from the assessment video in January. They were wistful, reflective pieces and latterly we had played them on Cara's CD player at her bedtime. We also included two songs by the African Children's Choir, which Cara had loved when she had seen them at our old church because of the complex rhythms and energetic, colourful dancing.

The Sunday before Cara's death, I had been too spent to go to church and had listened to a service from somewhere in Northern Ireland on the radio. One of the hymns was the modern worship song by Matt Redman, 'Blessed Be Your Name (in the land that is plentiful)'. It was beautifully arranged and sung, and throughout Cara's time in the hospital it played in my head, especially the lines that said:

Blessed be your name
on the road marked with suffering,
Though there's pain in the offering
blessed be your name.

We chose that song to begin the service, and Graham Kendrick's 'Make Way, Make Way (for Christ the King)' as the recessional. It was a good note to finish on, because it had a triumphant tune that was well known and it looked forward, as we always had during Cara's lifetime, to Christ's new world of wholeness and justice for everyone.

Undoubtedly, we orchestrated it carefully, with Rosalyn's help and considerable input. The bit of me that recognizes the point of drama wanted to allow room for the expression of real emotion, to touch people with the tragedy and hope inherent in what had happened, rather than allowing them to pay lip-service to mourning and creep away in embarrassment. I think a number of people, including David's mother, were slightly apprehensive about what was going to take place, but on the day, it meant that there were lots of people in the church, waiting to observe how Christianity dealt with this particular story and what it had to say, if anything.

And that was a slight problem. We didn't want the funeral to become a political event, with council managers who barely knew Cara turning up to save face. As it happened, the divisional head of social services called us, and I was able to ask him to convey our wishes that no-one who hadn't worked directly with Cara should come.

Allie called David to ask if there was anything she could do. David politely directed her to call OT and inform them what had happened. Then she asked about when the funeral was to take place. David paused.

'You don't want me to come, do you?' she said, displaying for her a rare level of perception.

'Well, no, actually, we don't,' said David quietly. 'Rhona is feeling pretty fragile at the moment and I don't think it would be helpful.'

In retrospect, it seems a bit mean, but at the time, I don't think I could have coped. Our confidence and trust in Allie had broken down to such an extent that our relationship with her caused only distress, rather than support.

As the funeral plans progressed, and Ernie the undertaker continued to liaise with us, David continued to liaise with the hospital. I had originally wanted to send a pretty party dress for Cara to wear, but when Ernie knew there was to be a post-mortem, he said very gently that it would be better to leave her in the hospital's pink pyjamas and not interfere too much with her. On the day the post-mortem was to take place, we went to Saltwell Park, where Charis played in the sand pit, our dog did lots of socializing with the park's canine population and we tried not to think what was happening to Cara's body as we were enjoying the sunshine. For many parents, this would have been the final straw, but nothing about our life with Cara had ever been normal.

We wanted to know, in any case, what had happened, just as much as the doctors and the authorities did, and if a post-mortem could shed any light on what had been wrong with Cara throughout her life, we also wanted to know, as much for Charis's possible future children as for our own peace of mind.

I thought of Cara sitting in heaven, smiling her beautiful, enigmatic smile and chuckling that deep, robust chuckle at all of us desperately trying to find out what we could never fathom during her life. 'I don't think anyone will ever know,' I said to David and my mother. 'I think she will be as much a mystery in death as she was in life.'

And so it proved. When the hospital finally called David's mobile, the pathologist was willing to offer only tentative conclusions as to the cause of death, citing her epilepsy as a major factor, and a urinary tract infection leading to possible septicaemia. This would allow the hospital to release the body for an interim death certificate and cremation, but might eventually lead to an inquest. In the end, about six months later, the coroner accepted the findings of the pathologist and ruled that an inquest would probably be equally inconclusive.

We thought often of what an acquaintance of ours, an orthopaedic surgeon, had said when he visited us in the week after Cara's death: 'At the end of the day, the Lord called her home.' And I still think of her laughing at having outwitted all of us and, with a child's instinct and the Lord's help, having neatly sidestepped all the issues surrounding her life and plunging, a free girl at last, into a life better than anything we could have given her.

We continued to open the cards that arrived daily, and which in the end numbered over seventy. We had visits from a number of people; some were welcome, some not quite so much. Cara's teacher at Coquet Vale turned up one evening because he would not be able to attend the funeral, and we chatted civilly. However, the senior social worker also came to visit us. David was much better than I was at dealing with it; I stayed quiet until she said that it must be some comfort to me that Cara had died without feeling pain or suffering. Then, tearful, furious and pushed to the limit, I told her exactly what I thought of the job that was currently being done by people who were supposed to make the lives of the disabled better, not worse. I stalked off upstairs, leaving her in tears and David picking up the pieces, and the incident brought me back from the safe, insulated world of grief and comfort, and at least temporarily into desolation. After she had gone, I went out to scrape the moss from the drive, eviscerating each crevice savagely until the anger ebbed away.

The day dawned, a sunny, late-summer day that meant that nothing would be complicated by the weather. My mother arrived early and helped us to get Charis ready; she would be wearing her best dress, a pretty, coral broderie anglaise little girl's dress that almost matched her hair and that would be a bright note among all the dark colours. Fiona and Rachel, from my prayer group, were going to take her downstairs to play in the crèche area if she became too restless; she was, after all, only two and a half and really had very little idea of what was happening.

We both managed to cope quite well until the flowers arrived, and as they were placed on the lawn, David had to go out into the garden for a while to recover his self-control. Then, about mid-morning, the family started to arrive: David's mother and her partner Robert, David's brother Ian and his new wife Kelly who had been getting married in Florida during Cara's last illness, and whom we hadn't told until they came back, because we didn't want to spoil their honeymoon. They were accompanied by Jack, Ian's younger son from his first marriage.

Then the cars came, one for us, and one containing the little white coffin with the spray of flowers. That was one of the hardest parts for me, sitting in the big black taxi watching the last I would ever see of Cara in this life as we sped towards Durham and St Nic's.

Rosalyn was waiting for us outside and she hugged me before we went in. Charis, seeing Cara's face on the overhead projector, exclaimed 'There's Cara!' and there was a ripple of faint laughter and comment. I had the impression of a church that was almost full, and a variety of faces from many different parts of Cara's life: neighbours, people who had helped with her physio programme, friends from the past, friends from our old church and from St Nic's, care-workers that I knew, and other faces that I didn't recognize at all. We took our seats in the front row, and the service began.

I was surprised that I was able to make the responses and sing when required. That was probably due to the need to do the last things we could for Cara, and also the need to show those around us that we weren't mourning without hope, that our grief was real, but so was our faith. I listened to the words of the service, beautiful, dignified and utterly relevant, a grown-up way of dealing with death. The phrase that sticks most in my mind is the one that proclaimed that Cara had passed from 'limitation to wholeness', because that was what we had wanted for her all her life, and even as my eyes were full of tears, I smiled faintly. Everyone was completely silent as we watched the video that David had so lovingly assembled, and the saxophone accompaniment took away some of the intensity and allowed people to relax even as they stayed aware of the solemnity of the occasion.

Rosalyn stepped forward, gave the slight nod of the head and pursing of the lips that were characteristic of her, and began her sermon. She talked about Cara and she drew together the threads of the readings, saying that, whatever our need and whatever he chooses to do in response to it, Jesus doesn't provide the answer – he *is* the answer; that he is able to move in our lives for good if we let him and surrender our own desires to his purposes and the building of his kingdom. She talked about her son-in-law, a medical researcher, and the hope and despair that attended his work; she commended all of us who were engaged in trying to build the kingdom – parents, doctors, careworkers, teachers – but left us in no doubt that God expected the very best of us, because whether we chose to acknowledge it or not, we were doing his work. She referred to Cara's life now – that it had not ended, but continued, that she was now blessedly free from her infirmities, that the parting was not permanent. 'And when we see her again,' she said, making eye contact and smiling at everyone, 'she will be glorious!'

There was a palpable lightening of the atmosphere, and the congregation seemed to enter into her hope and joy. 'But for now,' she continued, 'our work is not finished. We say goodbye to Cara and we are sent back to build the kingdom. Let us do this in the awareness that Jesus is with us.'

As the coffin bearers took their places, the organist swept us into 'Make Way', and the whole church was carried along by the message of hope in the song. Rosalyn said to me afterwards that she felt that it was almost like saying, 'Make way, Cara's coming!' I felt that we could never have chosen a more appropriate hymn, even though, whenever it features in a service now, I find it hard to sing it because I associate it with that day.

I actually wanted to stay to the end, but we had to follow the coffin outside into the sunshine and get into the car. Mike, Alex's husband, who was on the sound desk, told us that the final piece of music, even though they had had problems with it, played perfectly to end the service. I was happy about that; it was *'Inye Watato'* ('Lord, take our hands in case we fall'), a piece by the African Children's Choir, an explosion of joy and confidence in God, full of drums and vocal effects and ending with the name *Yesu* repeated several times.

We relaxed a little in the car on the way to the crematorium, which wasn't far, and then quietly followed the coffin again inside the small chapel. The sun shone through the stained-glass window and lit up the cross on the altar as Rosalyn, with dignity and authority, led the prayers before committal; it seemed that the Lord was providing his own special effects.

The last piece of music we had chosen was 'You Are the Shepherd', a quiet, simple song written especially for that particular group of children who formed the choir from South Africa, many of whom were AIDS orphans. We had seen the little girl who sang the solo, Nomfundo, perform the song at our old church with the other children, and the performance had lost none of its utter sincerity and innocence by being recorded. David's mother clasped both our hands as the coffin began to move from our view, but we were not distressed by it. Cara had already gone; we would not cling to what was left.

There was a short silence after the song had finished, and then we heard a further piece of music, the Intermezzo from *Cavalleria Rusticana*, calming, slow, bringing everyone gradually back, and we stared at the sunlit cross. I thought this music was just something the crematorium played as a matter of course, but we discovered later that Rosalyn had been so overcome after 'You Are the Shepherd' that she had been unable to speak for a few minutes.

Outside, we talked quietly with those who had come to see the final act. Cara's careworkers were there; funerals were very much part of the job for them, but they hadn't been to one quite like this before.

Back at the church, our house group slipped smoothly into the role of waiting on those who had stayed behind to eat and talk with us. After it was over, we went back home, and I immediately lay down on our bed and slept for about three hours.

The day drew to a close as I watched television and saw an episode of *Who Do You Think You Are?* featuring Natasha Kaplinsky. The programme ended with her cousin standing in a deserted synagogue in Belarus, singing the Jewish prayers for the dead for those members of the family who had lost their lives in the Nazi occupation. Her cousin was a plain, balding, square-faced man, but he had a fine tenor voice, and the prayer was note-perfect. The yearning cadences of the tune juxtaposed with the triumphant proclamation of the words, taken from Job: 'Glorified and praised be the name of the Lord!', and summed up our day perfectly.

# 13 Afterwards

The weeks went on, and we began to re-establish a routine without Cara. David eventually underwent a phased return to work, and I returned to the various things I had done with Charis while Cara had been at school: toddler groups, prayer group, shopping, housework. The one thing that changed radically was that at first I stayed out of the house in the afternoons until after the time when Cara used to come home from school, because the dog would jump up at every noise. It took me a long time also not to feel that I had to get things ready for the careworkers to come in the mornings.

I had to come to terms with the reality of how exhausted I was and how that had been the case for many months before Cara's death. It was as if, like a cartoon character, I had run out far beyond the edge of a precipice and it was only once I looked down that I saw how far away I was from safety. I took my medication obediently, saw my doctor on a regular basis and tried hard not to be tormented by the stabbing sense of loss that throbbed in my heart like a sewing-machine needle and from time to time rose up like an iceberg in my head. I knew that Cara was OK – that was a given – but it couldn't stop the pain altogether. Gradually, the emotions ebbed and it was almost like being bereaved of the bereavement – as if Cara herself had moved on and had truly left us at last.

We had lots of positive comments about the funeral, mostly from people who didn't normally go to church, or who usually attended free churches. I don't think anyone had expected that the good old 'C. of E.' could produce something so creative and relevant in response to such a tragedy. Some said how much food for thought it had given them, and Rosalyn herself said that she felt that the Holy Spirit had very much been working on the day. One of Cara's social services carers told Janet our childminder, in a chance encounter, that she had actually enjoyed the service, and the general sense in David's family, none of whom were regular churchgoers, was that it had been very uplifting. Even now, we like to look back on it as something that was very positive and helpful, and that helped us to make sense of things.

To some people, both within and outside the church, we may not appear to be very good adverts for Christianity. We didn't behave like saints, and in almost everything we tried to achieve for Cara, we failed: we couldn't make her better, we didn't get the help from the education system we tried to get, and we couldn't even manage to make the local authority give us appropriate facilities for Cara at home. But I am comforted by an awareness that has only recently begun to dawn on me: that God does not always require us to be successful: he requires us to be faithful. The outcome of what we do is not wholly in our hands, and the story isn't yet over. The comfort that we have is that in faith, however imperfectly, we did everything that we were asked to do as Cara's parents and advocates.

We were part of a cause that we now know was much bigger than Cara and ourselves. That is hard to recognize, especially when a beloved child is involved who appears to be suffering because of the particular injustice that is being opposed. But if it hadn't affected us as directly as it did, I very much doubt if we would have fought so hard, or spoken to so many people, from ordinary acquaintances, to local authority officials, to the Ombudsman, to Members of Parliament. To however limited a degree, we had some impact on hearts and minds. It is scant comfort, but it is some comfort.

In the early days, when I was watching the God Channel, I recall Joyce Meyer discussing apparently unanswered prayers and saying that if, for whatever reason, God does not bless you in one area of your life, he will pour out his blessings in another. The great medieval mystic Mother Julian of Norwich believed that God does not always choose to answer us in the way we want because he intends for us 'more grace, or a better time, or a better gift'.[1] The psalmist, in Psalm 103:2, tells us to bless God and 'forget not all his benefits' (AV). If God does not always work things out exactly as we wish, we can be absolutely certain that he will show his love to us by other means.

We were always blessed materially and never had to struggle seriously to live as so many families with disabled children have to do; David's work has prospered beyond that of many other people, and we were given a miracle in Charis's birth and continuing health that overturned every bad expectation. Whereas, from the beginning, everything went wrong for Cara, every medical obstacle was overcome for Charis. I don't know why God chose to allow it to happen in that way. I just live with the mystery and am thankful for the child I still have.

No-one, even now, can explain why Cara was born as she was, so I won't attempt to give any easy, supposedly spiritual answer either. The present Archbishop of Canterbury, Dr Rowan Williams, once caused consternation when he compared Christ on the cross to a spastic child; for parents like us, to liken Christ to an object of pity, horror and utter helplessness is entirely appropriate: in his birth and in his death, Jesus chose to identify himself with the weakest, the most needy and, to ordinary human eyes, the least attractive.

Suffering with Cara opened our lives to God's grace in a way that would not have been possible otherwise. We learned patience, endurance, hope and compassion for others, as well as acquiring a deep knowledge of our own limitations and failings. Because of our constant need to fight against the darkness and corruption in those systems that denied Cara her opportunities, we also learned at a deep level that evangelical Christians need to be involved in issues of social justice as our nineteenth-century forebears were, rather than believing that evangelistic programmes, however important they are, should be the exclusive Christian answer to every social problem.

We also learned that the larger and more popular matters of justice that engage the attention of the media, such as fair trade and climate change, are by no means the only areas where Christians must seek to extend the kingdom; some of us are called to do so in council offices, in school classrooms, in private and hidden exchanges that may affect only a handful of people and that will never make it into the news. We weren't so much called as compelled into our particular cause, and for others, both the nature of the call and the work given to them may be very different from ours, but I do believe that it is something that all Christians need to support each other in doing.

In January, we again picked up the threads of Cara's case with the Ombudsman's office. David, in particular, was very anxious to make clear the difficulties we had suffered. After much discussion, we were finally granted a personal interview with the Ombudsman herself, accompanied by one of her investigators, so we drove down to York one morning armed with presentation material and an awareness that, regardless of whether anything could be done, we wanted to flag up some of the flaws in the current system.

We were listened to with great respect and told that the information we had provided about Sunderland's SEN shortcomings would certainly be borne in mind in relation to cases where there was clear evidence of ongoing failure to deliver a statement. However, we were also told that the Ombudsman's powers had been greatly curtailed by recent case law and that there was little that she could do.

Since we were not going to be given legal aid and didn't have the money to sue the LEA, Cara's case effectively had nowhere to go. The Ombudsman did not have the powers; Ofsted, which had recently described Cara's last school as 'Very Good', didn't want to make waves; and the school governors who had presided over the school that had failed her saw no need for change. In all our years of fighting, we had wondered why things were so bad: now we knew. It was because most of the people in charge of trying to make things better either did not have the powers to do so, or chose not to use the powers they had. The 'machine' did not allow dissidents to be taken seriously and did not consider it worthwhile to bring people to book for failure to comply with the law. And this was endemic, from government quangos like SENDIST and Ofsted, from the highest levels of local education authorities, down to the levels of the school governors. We had been voices crying in the wilderness all along when we had wanted the state to be concerned about Cara.

If the maintaining of systems is more important than the need to help the individuals for whom the systems are set up, then why are they there at all? So that society can maintain the fiction that it is acting humanely, when in fact it is discriminating hugely against a group of vulnerable human beings who are incapable of demanding better treatment? If parents of disabled children are sincerely required to work in partnership with educational and health service professionals, then why are those professionals often so resistant to a two-way dialogue that might achieve some results? And if the systems in place are not really working very satisfactorily, then why do the professionals insist on maintaining them and strongly resist any form of innovation or change, even to the point where they victimize the people they are allegedly trying to help? These are unanswerable questions when examined in the light of common sense.

We knew we would probably be given a carefully argued series of reasons about why the Ombudsman's office could not do anything much about the failures in Cara's education. However, when we talked also about the difficulties we had had with the local authority's procrastination and incompetence in relation to home facilities, we were told that it was possible for something to be done about this if we submitted another case.

We were right in assuming that nothing could be done about the LEA. The letter, a lengthy document, arrived about a fortnight later. I didn't read it in its entirety then and I still haven't. Instead, I sat down one Sunday afternoon and spent five hours putting together a case about the extension. Then, I finally put my brain into neutral for a while, and did nothing for about four months. Our complaint was eventually upheld – but the limited powers of the Ombudsman had precluded her office from doing very much to rectify matters. The local authority offered us £1,000 by way of compensation, which we refused, and the Ombudsman's office promised to keep an eye on the progress of the changes they had recommended the council to adopt.

It was a typically unsatisfactory outcome, but that was it. I wrote an impassioned and strongly worded letter to the Ombudsman's office, and after a great deal of internal conflict, mentally closed the book, as much for my own sanity as for any other reason.

We have passed the first anniversary of Cara's death and much has happened since those terrible and dreamlike weeks, when her battle and ours finally ended. From living in an intense, very high-pressure bubble that at times seemed to seal us off hermetically from the rest of the world, our lives are moving towards what could be called normality.

Charis is now three, a typical toddler with a strong will and an outgoing, friendly disposition, who expects the world to be a good place in which doing the right thing brings rewards, and doing the wrong one brings correction. It is sometimes hard for us to continue to teach her what all good parents try to teach their children, when our view of what the world is like has been so distorted by our experiences with her sister.

David has changed jobs and I am planning to do a law course. I see that as my part in building the kingdom: to use the skills I discovered when I was Cara's mother to try to make a better world for children like her. The redemption that I wanted for Cara has become a much wider picture and one that I hope will touch many people. I look forward to a new life that uses the experiences and lessons of the old one; always in faith, I anticipate what comes next without forgetting what has been.

I think a lot about forgiveness, because without it, I think I would be spending my whole life devoured by pain and mistrust. I believe that forgiveness is a decision, not an emotion. If part of forgiveness is to refrain from seeking revenge and to refrain from constantly dwelling on the failures of individuals to the point where the problems of the past become the dictator of my future actions and responses, then I have consciously chosen to do this and to move forward, trusting God to take care of the rest.

While I know that forgiveness in the end must be unconditional, I have observed that people often find forgiveness easier when there has been recognition of the wrong that was done, and some attempt to redress this wrong. To date, no-one in the council has acknowledged that we had legitimate grievances that were not dealt with as well as they might have been. But I have, in the end, arrived at a level of acceptance and relative emotional neutrality that, nevertheless, does not deny the reality of the pain we suffered, or the things in the system that need to change, because this story is not just about Cara and us.

There are two very difficult and extreme expectations placed on Christians who have suffered at the hands of others; one is that we vow a lifetime vendetta, especially against those who harm our children; and the other, sadly, is from many Christians, who really would prefer it if all the messy emotions were somehow instantly swept into a kind of bland, robot-like acceptance. Some Christians prefer not to think of God in terms of judging wrongdoing, and shrink from the very idea of a final reckoning for those who do not repent of their sins. I don't believe that is a viewpoint that accurately reflects the teaching of Scripture.

Indeed, if we are not to pursue vengeance ourselves, then to know that God has such matters firmly in hand can be a considerable source of comfort to those who struggle at a deep personal level with the difficult and destructive negative emotions that accompany injustice. I once read an interview with the first woman regional chief constable, who happened to be a Christian, and who said that sometimes all that enabled her to deal with those times when hardened offenders yet again escaped the justice of the courts was the knowledge that, in the end, they would not be able to escape from God's justice. I don't waste my spare moments by dwelling on what may lie in store for those who knowingly prevented Cara from having her legal and moral rights, but I do, as Joel Edwards once said in a talk I heard, aspire to be able to look in the eye without anger those who have wronged me and mine, and to trust God to take care of business, however he chooses to do it. Surrendering my own deep commitment to my daughter's cause into God's hands after almost eleven long years of struggle has been hard, but doing so is a necessary part of moving on for me.

I also accept that what was done to Cara and to us cannot now be undone by any human agency, and that even if justice was to be granted, it would not wipe out the pain and the hurt, because only God himself can do that. I am willing to give God time to work out what has happened, and to trust that if I continue to love and follow him, forgetting what is past and allowing my pain to be hidden with him in Christ, he will orchestrate all things so that they work together for good.

As I write, it is Advent, the season when Christians not only remember the birth of Jesus, but anticipate the time when he will come again. As I have grown older, I have become more preoccupied with the latter: Jesus the Redeemer, the great, universal Lord of the ancient icons, the incarnation of Truth, the one who delivers justice and mercy, raises up the downtrodden and heals all wounds.

Come, Lord Jesus.

# Epilogue

Today would have been Cara's twelfth birthday and it is now almost three years since her death. Our journey from the world we inhabited then to a life more closely resembling normality has not always been easy, nor, I think, will it ever be possible for us to regain the life we had before Cara. This is particularly true for me, since, one way or another, most of my life was taken up with Cara, and there was little room for very much else. From her earliest days, throughout her physiotherapy and intelligence programmes, to our difficulties in securing a better deal for her, Cara was mainly my job, and I had no other.

We miss Cara, and are constantly reminded of her: in my case, whenever I see a child in a wheelchair, or see some toy I think she might have liked or some clothes she would have looked pretty in. We adore Charis, but there are times when our family feels incomplete, when we think of what might have been if Cara had been well, and when I think that, even if it were just for one day, I would love to have her back again and do the things we did before: to watch her play with her hoop, to smell her hair, and hear her deep explosive chuckle that was unique and more joyous than any laugh I have ever heard.

Although I thank God that I have another child to care for who enjoys good health, I do not experience the same intensity or anxiety that characterized my relationship with Cara, because Charis is a healthy child and simply does not need the same level of input, however much she is loved, nurtured and enjoyed. The playing field for Charis is considerably more level than it ever was for Cara, and the feeling of being constantly 'on duty' in every aspect of her life is absent.

The experience of being Cara's mother has marked me for almost ten years of my life. I am now less innocent and accepting of people and situations at face value, and more inclined to look beneath the surface. I am also much more willing to engage with authority in whatever form, because I know that no earthly authority is ever right all the time, and that no-one can or should be immune to question and challenge, though most of the time my questions are less fraught and urgent than they were on Cara's behalf.

Looking back, I can recognize some of the mistakes we made. It was both draining and sometimes counter-productive to be as unyielding as we eventually became. But through our resistance we gained for Cara some real, though limited, achievements. She had three years at a nursery and a school where she was very happy, and where her personality developed to the point where we could see something of the child she might have been if she had been well. This means a lot to us when her life in the end turned out to be so short. Because of our physiotherapy, Cara had several years of relatively good health and comfort. She seemed to be markedly healthier than other children with similar conditions, and these things alone make what we did worthwhile in our eyes.

The facts of Cara's life make this book seem very bleak at times – but to write it in a different way would be to betray not only the truth of our experiences, but also those people who are currently struggling with situations that are as bad as, if not worse than, ours was. The world of the disabled and their carers is to varying degrees a very hard one, regardless of whether or not they adopt the proactive stance we took, and I have tried to depict it honestly. In the end, I believe only the truth allows proper reflection and real change for the better.

We never felt that it was right for Cara, or anyone else's child, to be almost entirely dependent for their well-being on increasingly overstretched parent-carers, sporadic public goodwill and the uncertain tides of voluntary charity. This in my view can only be the alternative and the end result when parents do not participate in invoking their children's rights under the law. This is why we followed the road we did, not only for the sake of our own child, but because thereby we hoped to improve the lives of other children too. I did not think twice about whether it was 'right' to fight on Cara's behalf at the time, and I would do the same again, though I might try to be less angry and outspoken.

We believed, and always will, that God has a hope and a future for children like Cara, as he has a hope and a future for everyone, not only in the next world, but also in this one. To quote an old Christian Aid slogan, we believed in 'life before death' for her: a life of dignity, comfort, and fair and equal treatment. We always had hope for Cara, but felt that she was denied the future to which we aspired for her. Our own experiences painfully taught us to believe that such children are inherently disadvantaged by the current infra-structure, and that the law currently offers limited protection and assistance to them. It certainly seemed so to us. We continue periodically to watch in horror as a tiny minority of parents, who are unable to deal any longer with their situations and despair of what the future may hold, kill themselves and their children because they can see no other way out. There is something very wrong when people become as desperate as this.

The lesson I learned through becoming a 'disability activist' for Cara has, I believe, a wider application. It seems to me that if Christians were heard more often on day-to-day issues and in the small things, then it might be easier to be heard and understood when we take a stand on the big issues. We now live in a society where minorities are increasingly vocal in defence of their rights, and where it is therefore often assumed that silence equals agreement or apathy. I believe it is important for us to lose our reticence and learn to speak up and speak out when circumstances require it.

My younger daughter was recently disciplined at school for something that was not entirely her fault, and she did not receive support to tell her side of the story. Before Cara, I might have let this go, but we challenged it and sought appropriate dialogue with the school, with a favourable outcome and better understanding on both sides. My mother noticed that some motorists were routinely ignoring red lights at a school crossing during the morning rush hour. She had a quiet word with the head teacher, speed cameras were subsequently installed, and the problem ceased. The practice of good Christian citizenship and seeking to build God's kingdom can just as easily be about things as apparently insignificant as these as about taking a stand on much bigger, more overtly religious or more contentious issues. It can also involve affirming and supporting good initiatives as much as seeking to change bad ones.

The late Robert F. Kennedy, a significant figure in social justice whose political stance was consciously motivated and sustained by his Christian faith, asserted the importance of individual gestures on the side of justice:

Let no-one be discouraged by the belief that there is nothing one man or one woman can do against the enormous array of the world's ills . . . Each time a man stands up for an ideal, or acts to improve the lot of others, or strikes out against injustice, he sends forth a tiny ripple of hope.[1]

The challenge, if we accept it, means that it could be down to us whether or not children like Cara receive what we believe God wants for them: not only the certain hope of eternal life that is granted to them by Christ, but a future in this world that is worth having.

1 March 2010

# Appendix: Organizations

Brain-Net, the organization that helped us so much in the early years, is as far as I am aware now defunct; however, there are other organizations that provide forms of the Doman-Delacato therapy. One of these is Brainwave:

Brainwave South West
Huntworth Gate
Bridgwater
Somerset TA6 6LQ
United Kingdom
Tel. 01278 429089 www.brainwave.org.uk

It has a second centre:

Brainwave South East
Beechen House
16 Newland Street
Witham
Essex CM8 2AQ
United Kingdom
Tel. 01376 505290

The other organization that provided good advice on matters relating to Cara's education was:

Independent Parental Special Education Advice (IPSEA)
6 Carlow Mews
Woodbridge
Suffolk IP12 1EA
United Kingdom
Tel. 01394 446575 www.ipsea.org.uk

SCOPE helps families living with cerebral palsy, in particular (which wasn't Cara's situation), and can be found at:

6 Market Road
London
N7 9PW
England
United Kingdom
www.scope.org.uk

Through-the-Roof is a Christian organization that exists to support disabled people and their families:

PO Box 353
Epsom
Surrey
KT18 5WS
www.throughtheroof.org.uk

Many of these organizations have good websites that will provide any further information parents need.

# Notes

## Chapter 1 A New Life

1. These were Bonhoeffer's last words before his execution on 8 April 1945 at Flossenbürg concentration camp, Germany.

## Chapter 3 Fear and Hope

1. Glenn Doman, *What To Do About Your Brain-Injured Child* (Avery Publishing Group, 1994), p. 209.

## Chapter 4 The Alison Centre, Changes and Challenges

1. Keith Pennock, *Rescuing Brain-Injured Children* (2nd edn, Ashgrove Publishing, 1999).

## Chapter 5 Opening Moves

1. The dispute was deliberately allowed to drag on and on in the hope that we would give in. Legislation gives clear time-limits within which action must be taken by the LEA.

## Chapter 7 Tribunal and Aftermath

1. I should explain a little more about SENDIST. Every parent has one right of appeal against a local authority if they disagree with the designated school for a child with special

needs, or if they take issue with what is written up in the child's statement. They are allowed to contest one or all of the parts of the statement. We were contesting all of these: Part 2 because it did not describe Cara's problems accurately enough; Part 3 because it did not specify and quantify therapy provision; and Part 4 because we did not feel that any of the Sunderland schools had sufficient expertise in place to address her difficulties.

## Chapter 9 A Matter of Caring

1. I first saw these words written at the foot of a statue of St Thérèse in St Andrew's Roman Catholic Church, Worswick Street, Newcastle. For more information please see *The Story of a Soul* by St Thérèse of Lisieux, numerous editions of which are in print, and the main website: www.ewtn.com/Therese/Therese1.htm. There are numerous other Theresian websites following the tour of her relics in 2009.

## Chapter 10 Unless the Lord Builds the House

1. Dietrich Bonhoeffer, *The Cost of Discipleship* (SCM Canterbury Press, 2001).
2. Robert Llewelyn, ed., *Enfolded in Love: Daily Readings with Julian of Norwich* (Darton, Longman and Todd, 1980), p. 59.
3. This is a complaints procedure at the highest level possible for a local authority before the Ombudsman is approached.

## Chapter 13 Afterwards

1. Robert Llewelyn, ed., *Enfolded in Love: Daily Readings with Julian of Norwich* (Darton, Longman and Todd, 1980), p. 22.

## Epilogue

1. Senator Robert F. Kennedy quotation from University of South Africa, National Union of South African Students' 'Day of Affirmation' Speech, 6 June 1966.